SHAPE UP
YOUR GOLF

SHAPE UP
YOUR GOLF

Sarah Sanderson

CollinsWillow

An Imprint of HarperCollins*Publishers*

First published in 2002 by
CollinsWillow
an imprint of HarperCollins*Publishers*
London

Text © Sarah Sanderson 2002

9 8 7 6 5 4 3 2 1

A CIP catalogue record for this book is available from the British Library.

ISBN 0 00 711580 6

Colour reproduction by Digital Imaging
Printed and bound in Italy by Johnson Editorial Ltd.

The HarperCollins website address is www.fireandwater.com

This book was created by
SP Creative Design
Sarah's Folly, Wickham Skeith, Suffolk
Editor: Heather Thomas
Art director: Rolando Ugolini

Photography by Dave Cannon
Additional photographs: Brendan Malone of ActionImages, page 9 (left), 132, 136;
Allsport, 6, 7 (bottom), 13, 25, 27, 31, 32, 39 (bottom), 40, 47, 53, 75, 80, 82, 83, 95, 98,
103, 107, 119, 121, 125, 126, 128, 130, 131, 133, 135, 138, 139, 141, 144, 145, 146, 152,
155; Hampshire Sport, 160; Andy Reddington, 9 (right), 142, 151

Contents

Foreword

By concentrating on the short game, how to get out of trouble, and developing a tough mental approach, this book tackles three really important elements to playing good golf.

Part of my trademark in the game has been the ability to play successful recovery shots which would prove virtually impossible for the majority of golfers to replicate. For instance, I would not have beaten Colin Montgomerie at the Seve Trophy at Druids Glen in 2002 without producing those rescue shots at vital moments.

These shots are the result of a vivid imagination backed up by a strong mind which defines one's self-belief. Failure is not envisaged; if you feed your brain with even the slightest possibility of a mistake, you will not succeed. This is the mantra of Sarah Sanderson's book.

To become an extraordinary player of the short game, natural feel and touch must be second nature. Sarah says that I have 'an almost mystical talent' in this area, and I am convinced that my strong short game and mental determination have kept me competing and earning many praises to this day.

Seve Ballesteros

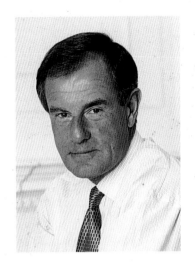

One of the most absorbing things about playing golf as a hobby is that whilst hitting a ball we can forget work for a few hours. However, this game that we all love can be so frustrating when our amateur brains think we can hit full shots like the pros – usually with disastrous results.

As Sarah suggests, developing a reliable short game and being able to escape from dire situations is invaluable to all part-time golfers. Golf is one of the few sports where business can be combined with pleasure. Certainly gamesmanship can come into play and it is absolutely true that boardroom tactics surface on the putting green. This is where a focused positive mental approach can make the difference between caving in to a lesser foe when they fail to give you that three-foot putt for the hole. Most amateurs lead busy lives with little time to practise. Using imagination and remembering to have fun can make those minutes spent putting on the office carpet pay dividends later out on the golf course.

Lord Ian MacLaurin Chairman of the England and Wales Cricket Board

My academy at Champions Gate, Orlando, has never seen the likes of Sarah. Leopards really do change their spots – she did so many wardrobe changes that photographer Dave Cannon had to practise his pitch shots in-between takes!

All coaches try to make golf teaching interesting and fun. It is always a battle to think up new ways of explaining the same techniques. This book certainly has a fresh approach at explaining the importance of a good short game and focused mind. Written by someone who leads a very varied life, it has twists in it that more conventional golf books do not. Practising your chip shots to cookery implements is a new one on me – anyone got a whisk I can borrow?

David Leadbetter

Introduction

Anyone who manages to connect with the golf ball at all should be proudly wearing a medal. The sadist who invented the idea of hitting a round object the size of a large free-range egg with a four-foot long stick will be howling with laughter at the agonies that most of us endure.

That one perfect shot, the holed 30-foot putt or a soaring drive, is the carrot dangling over us that keeps us hooked. This is one explanation for the reams of instruction manuals and teaching videos, all promising perfect professional results. Without these gems, we amateur golf addicts would have nothing to paw over with our Crunchy Nut Cornflakes at breakfast. Searching for yet another 'fix' becomes part of the fascination of playing golf.

The fundamental difference between a pro and the rest of us is that golf is their breadwinner. That alone alters the mindset for everything. On Tour there is no playtime, especially when one lapse in concentration means the mortgage skuttles out of the

conservatory. Armchair applause is all too rapidly supplanted with 'I could have sunk that!' as our pro slides one by from eight feet – but our gas and phone bills are not dependent on shooting a 68 in the final round. Whatever pressure we feel on our backswing is nothing compared to theirs.

Pro standards are rocket-launch high. 'Oh no, not another Par!' – just watch it on the box as their frustration boils over. How many of us would do backflips of joy if we could scribble Par, Par, Par, Par, oh and another boring Par, on our card? This translates into instruction. We are informed that on shots of 90 yards to the flag we should aim to end up five feet from the pin and sink the putt for birdie. How about just landing on the putting surface?

What I hope to do in this book is to act as mediator between how the pros view it and how we amateurs play the game. What's more, by concentrating on the short game and trying to develop a positive and constructive mental approach, I am confident that this will provide you with all that you need to produce top-notch golf.

CHAPTER ONE

What standard are you?

Think of all your friends who are either regular playing golfers, holiday punters, corporate guests or are considering taking up the game – it's quite a lot. Golf's handicap system categorizes us but it doesn't always reflect our actual playing ability. Some people only play once every three months; others, four times a week; and some only put in a card when it suits them in order to keep their handicap high, gaining more free shots. Par is the benchmark that all golf courses set against us. It ranges from 68 to 75 (ish) shots for 18 holes.

Use the handicap system

Amateurs come in four varieties and throughout this book, I shall refer to golfers in the following categories: Hackers, Club, Match, Scratch and Pro.

Hacker: 30+ over par

This is someone who has either played for a short time, or who plays very occasionally (half a dozen times a year). Rarely practising, they just want to knock the ball round without huge embarrassment – perhaps playing in a corporate golf day once or twice a year. There is also the person who, although earnestly striving for a better standard, feels that he or she has reached their golfing ceiling.

Pondering over a host of unnatural actions, it is surprising that sweet shots are still produced. Limitless joy is brought to the hacker by that one perfect strike in a round (conveniently erasing the memory of seven whacks out of a bunker!). For hackers, the effortless striking of scratch golfers might as well be on Mars.

Club: 10–30 over par

Mr, Mrs and Miss C (Club) pick up the prizes at golf days by entering 'invitationals', 'mixed gruesomes', 'something in aid of' and special seasonal scrambles – 'Turkey Trots'. Committee member, county delegate, rules official or competition organiser can all be part of a club member's life.

The ball flies where it's meant to go fairly often and reasonably well, even if the higher end of this category has to constantly think through the mechanics of the stroke. 'Pivot fully, keep the head steady, weight on the right – weight on the left – and through'. For them, effortless striking is only on the Moon.

Match: 4–9 over par

The match player is probably a seasoned golfer. They may have been better, but due to life commitments (or an ability block) cannot shave those last few shots off their scores to make it down to scratch. Junior or Colt members are often found in this category and, distractions permitting (parties, alcohol, 'trendier' pursuits, exams), they are still on the 'way down'. Representing the club's A side, county squad and entering national tournaments are all part of the challenges a single-figured amateur experiences.

There are then two levels that most of us will never reach – Scratch and Pro.

Scratch: 0–3 over par

Only featuring on club boards for scratch (gross score) competitions, they will probably wear the crown of club champion at some point. They are absolutely capable of representing a county side (although it is much harder for men than women). A scratch handicap is quite rare; it holds a certain cachet and some players will have country caps.

Pro

Teaching and playing, it's their job. Most golfers will never aspire to these dizzy heights.

Changing category

As time goes on, lessons learnt and practice spent, our category will change direction. This will alter several times during a golfing life. Sadly, the older we get, the higher our handicap is likely to rise as distance, particularly off the tee, diminishes. Conversely, if the game is taken up late, retirement can come to the rescue and the handicap comes tottering down.

How amateur are you?

We all have different approaches and aims in practice (some of us being allergic to the concept altogether!). The results 'on course' are directly linked to what, how and when we work on our game. A tired body with a brain that robotically repeats chip shots without concentrating on what is really going on, are better off with the feet up watching 'AbFab' or 'Who wants to be a Millionaire' on the box.

On the flip side, practice can be stress therapy, as after a bad day at the office it is far better to bash balls hypnotically than microwave the family hamster. To the hardy person just taking up the game, stare at the ball much longer than you think necessary – and, post-golf, be prepared to fall asleep on the sofa, knackered. It's to do with fresh air and brain cell usage.

The amateur game has changed and the era of the true amateur playing for their country is 'like a dog with two tails – very rare' (Blackadder).

Beware the Senior Houdini

Advancing years should not affect the short game. Many a good old hacker has a sharp one, and the seniors are notorious for taking four or five shots to reach the edge of the green and then playing like Merlin as they chip in or leave it dead.

Liquor and Longevity

The horse and mule live thirty years
    And nothing know of wines and beers.
The goat and sheep at twenty die
    And never taste of Scotch or Rye.
The cow drinks water by the ton
    And at eighteen is mostly done.
The dog at fifteen cashes in
    Without the aid of rum and gin.
The cat in milk and water soaks
    And then in twelve short years it croaks.
The modest, sober, bone-dry hen
    Lays eggs for nogs, then dies at ten.
All animals are strictly dry:
    They sinless live and swiftly die;
But sinful, ginful, rum-soaked men
    Survive for three score years and ten.
And some of them, a very few,
    Stay pickled till they're ninety-two.

Anon

Different types of player

Girls v Boys, Juniors v Seniors, Right v Left handers, differences of sex, age and dexterity affect the way we learn and play our golf. However, modern clubs empower the weaker armed, and age concerns have been 'Botoxed' smoothly out. With short shots, emulating the 'suck-back' effect of professional backspin is better left to those who can hit the ball straight on a regular basis.

Apologies to all you left-handed wizards out there. Still in the minority, you'll have to use your imagination when, for example, 'Open your left foot towards the target' is suggested.

Before you waggle a club

Here are some answers to questions that are commonly asked by newcomers who are thinking of taking up the game of golf.

Does golf take a long time to play?

It shouldn't – three to four hours is average. Play 9 hole loops if you can, or find a gap to 'push in on' and cut a few holes out. Signs of addiction show when you keep on until 'owl light' and notch up 39 holes in one session.

Is it expensive?

It doesn't have to bankrupt you; try investing in some secondhand clubs. Fourteen clubs is the official maximum number you can carry in your bag. Try a half set. One month, take the 'evens' (4, 6, 8, wedge, sand iron, putter, woods) and then swap them around. Put them in an old-fashioned slim bag, sling them over your back and prance along the fairways.

Is it too technical for me?

You've guessed it – no. Develop a personal system for 'get me out of trouble' shots. Have lessons, get a conventional swing sussed and use the text book, but experiment with what works for you, too – use your nous.

Left: Michael Hoey of Northern Ireland in action during the British Amateur Championships. Every amateur sport has become more professional in manner, and golf is no exception.

CHAPTER TWO

Putting

Putting is a huge part of the game and makes a very significant contribution to the score. It is easy to link it with money, because when most of us watch or listen to professional golf, even if only during Open week, we are regularly reminded by commentators that 'this putt is worth x zillion pounds'.

Your gilt-edged investment

This is the longest chapter in the book – and it should be, because 43 per cent of the entire game is putting. Whether it's a £10 million professional golf tournament, or our £1 a corner Saturday morning four-ball, the money at stake will primarily be won, lost or indeed saved – on the putting green. Invest in your putting!

Learn from back to front

Of course, we need to learn and refine a good full golf swing. However, if we were to spend considerable time early on in our golfing lives, working on putting, chips and pitches – the little shots first – we would witness a real difference when we came to trying to score well. Why is this so?

● Putting is technically the simplest stroke; from crazy golf punters to two-year-olds, they can all have a go at it (this doesn't necessarily mean they'll be any good). Putting is back and through – simple.

● Chipping is the next step up from putting; with little or no wrist action and a quiet lower body, it should be easy to grasp.

● Go back in distance and pitches are the natural successor to chips. With a small amount of body rotation, keeping hands, arms and torso 'connected' through the swing, pitches lead us towards the full shot.

If, instead of hammering balls with a wild slash of something resembling a full golf swing, we purposely stayed with putting and chips for 80 per cent of our practice time, we would get much better, quicker. It's human nature to do the opposite of this. But developing control of the club early on with the small shots and feeling how the club face responds first, is how we should go about it.

Drive for show but putt for dough!

Learn from the stats

Putting analysis tells us that we should spend much longer working on our putting and that short putts are missed more often than thought – by everyone. Let's work on distance judgement, since on putts over 20 feet we leave ourselves in 3 putt country far too often.

Right: My eyes are shut in this picture as I listen for the 'plop' of the ball going into the hole!

Strokes taken as putts

Forty three per cent (plus or minus two per cent) of the golf score is putting (Dave Peltz's *Putting Bible*) – a frightening statistic when you analyse how little time we spend on our putting. Perfectly content with the state of the day's play, we return to the clubhouse, calculator in hand, to discover that our score was 'nay quite as good' as we thought – and all down to exceeding budget on the 'dance floor'. The up-side is that if you are a green magician, you will profit – and it takes far less effort to downsize putting scores than to control wayward driving.

Putt well and win

Believe it or not, 55 per cent of all first putts of six feet are missed by the pros playing in PGA tournaments – and they concentrate, practise and perform on super-smooth surfaces. When did you last hear of a pro

C-o-n-c-e-n-t-r-a-t-e
Make a proper putting stroke...
even for the tiny putts

whining about tine-marks or temporary greens? Furry winter surfaces are something they never face – they're too busy sunning it in Dubai, California or 'Down Under'.

Long putts: judging length

If the worst you do is to make a 10 per cent error on the length of most long putts, regardless of line, you should still two putt (this positions you inside the average three putt zone of 2 feet from the hole). If you make a 10 per cent error on the line of most long putts, regardless of length, you are likely to three putt. Even being 90 per cent on line (and most of us are not total idiots and can aim the ball reasonably accurately), if 90 per cent of the distance to the hole is not judged correctly, getting down in two will be left to chance.

Improve your score

You could improve your score by an average of five shots per round if you:
● Holed most four footers
● Judged the length of long ones (20 plus feet) dead, cutting down on three putts, and
● Used mathematics, e.g. 10 per cent of 20 ft = 2 ft = tap-in.
This would reduce the percentage of your game spent on putting below 43 per cent.

Hike in the profits

Parting with hard-earned cash for the fortnightly couch session with the pro for endless swing check-ups can become addictive. The swing must be learnt and then honed, but investing in championing these putts is the golfing equivalent of the carpet-bagging investor cornering the building societies – short-term activity for long-term profit. So cut down on percentage misses by fine-tuning your putting.

Above: Judging length is always very important, especially on the long putts.

Let's get back to basics

Most of us will have formed a putting stroke, and some of us will have had it for many years. However, it is still worthwhile going back to basics every now and then and checking out the fundamentals of putting.

Posture

● Your knees should be slightly flexed.
● Bend from the waist with your arms hanging down.
● Practise cupping your hands (without holding the club). By doing this, your hands are able to swing more easily in a classic putting pendulum motion.

Stance and ball position

● Your feet should be shoulder width apart.
● Put the ball wherever you like; just make it comfortable. The norm is: either middle or towards the left forward foot as it aids forward roll.
● Keep your weight centred – or slightly on your left side.

Below: **Without the club, cup your hands as if you are about to give a friend a foot up. (This way, your hands are able to swing easily in a pendulum motion.)**

Right: **When setting up for a putt, pay special attention to posture. Your knees should be slightly flexed and you should bend from the waist. Position the ball in the middle of the stance or towards the left foot.**

Grip

There are endless variables when it comes to gripping the putter: fingers down, fingers curled, etc. With all grips, the main point is to have light pressure as it cultivates feel, which is what good putting is all about. The majority of us will stick with convention and work at the basic putting style but, as we shall see, there are lots of other idiosyncratic options.

Basic grip

The grip is a highly personal thing and you need to find out what works best for you. At this stage in the 'back to basics' exercise, use your existing grip or just hold the club with both hands. If you're a beginner, place the left hand on the club first, and then slide the right hand up to join it. Curl your right little finger around your left forefinger.

Above from left to right: **To build the basic putting grip, place your left hand on the club first. Now slide the right hand up the shaft to join the left one, curling your right little finger around your left forefinger.**

Right: The side-saddle style of putting is quite rare and idiosyncratic – not to be recommended.

Side-saddle grip

This style should be accredited to Sam Snead and croquet. Originally, the ball was hit from between the legs with a special putter acting just like a mallet. The Royal & Ancient God Squad decided this was not on and wrote the 11th Commandment, banning it. Sam then put his feet together and went 'side-saddle' – and carried on sinking putt after putt.

Light pressure = feel

How hard should the club be gripped? Imagine that you've got a peeled, over-ripe, banana in your hands. Hold the banana solidly yet sensitively enough to ensure you don't end up with bits oozing between the fingers.

Grip the shaft of the club in the palms of your hands – not like a full swing grip, which allows the wrists to flex. We want solid wrists with little or no wrist action. The longer the putt, the more wrist break there will be.

Broomhandle grip

This is not just a change in grip but a new style with a new length putter. The advantage to the broomhandle is that it neutralizes any wrist action. The left hand holds the club as you would grasp a microphone in the fingers, and the right hand acts as a guide for balance and direction with two fingers on the shaft.

The advantages of this grip are as follows: no more backache; it's easy on the nervous system; once the technique is mastered, the pendulum action takes over; and it's very good on medium to short length putts as the wrists are taken out of the equation. The disadvantages are: long range putting can be quite stilted when wielding such a long implement; and it's hopeless squeezing one into the boot of a Porsche.

Ambidextrous grip

If you play right-handed, try putting left-handed with a left-handed putter. Notah Begay III pro putts left- and right-handed, depending on the break of the putt. Even if

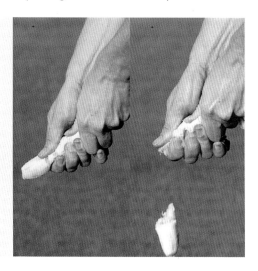

this is not for you, it is a worthwhile exercise as it forces you to think hard about alignment, grip and stroke. Sergio Garcia takes this idea to extremes and can play most shots perfectly with right- and left-handed clubs – lucky, over-talented Spanish personage.

'Cack-handed' or reverse grip

Using this grip, the left hand is below the right (vice-versa for left handers). Have a go. It's as if the left shoulder has been yanked down.

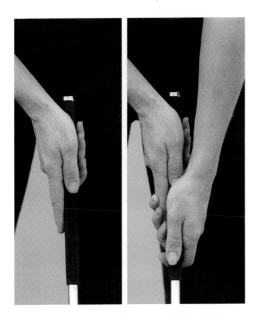

Above: For the reverse grip, put the left hand below the right and you'll feel just how solid, almost stiff, the hands become.

Little or no wrist action

Keep an even pressure on the grip, otherwise you risk unpredictable changes in the speed of the putter head and loss of direction. If the right hand becomes dominant, it can pull or push the putt. As most of us are right-handed, this is a mistake to watch out for.

Aim

● Get the putter face *square* to the hole – not open (to the right) or shut (to the left). It should be at 90 degrees to the hole.
● With your feet either side of the ball, draw an imaginary line to the hole across the toes, which runs parallel to the hole.
● Adjust your stance until the line of the toes is parallel to the hole. After aiming, keep your head still.

Left: When aiming, the putter face should always be square to the hole. Try drawing an imaginary line across the end of your toes parallel to the hole and another from the centre of the ball to the hole.

Warning! There may be a tendency to turn the left foot out, which will give you an open stance, aiming left of the hole. Look at what your *heels* are doing. (Take the parallel horizontal line from your heels to the hole if you have a wandering left toe.)

Head and eye position

You should always keep your eyes right over the ball – it's the easiest way to see the line of the putt. Don't lift your head up and down when you're having a peek at the line – you aren't a mere cat!

Right: **You may swivel your head to the left or right along the putter line but don't lift it up and down.**

Pendulum swing

For the pendulum swing, you need to form an upside-down soft triangle shape from your elbows to your hands. This creates a good space to lead the stroke off – with a down on the left and up on the right shoulder tilt.

Sarah's soundbites

Snout sensor To check your eyes are in the right place over the ball, put a ball on the ground and stand as if you were about to putt but with no club. Make sure the ball is where you would usually putt the ball from. Hold another ball to the bridge of your nose and drop it. Objective: this ball should hit the one on the ground smack in the middle.

Lead with the hands and always keep the putter moving past your left forward knee towards the target. Stay down throughout this stroke – keep those eyes peeled on the ball, not on the club as it goes back. That way, you'll stay on line over the ball.

Below: For the pendulum swing, always lead with your hands and keep the putter moving towards the target. Watch the ball, not the club, as you take it back. To hold your putting posture throughout the stroke, don't move your whole head. You can follow the line of the putt by swivelling your eyes towards the hole.

Back and through... accelerate through impact

Cashing in

There are many ways to deposit the ball in the hole. Whether it plops, flips, creeps unwillingly or jumps wholeheartedly into the safe, we don't really care: we're in credit. However, you've got to admit, watching Tiger rattle and shake is exciting. That is real confidence for you. We want that confidence.

Opposite: Tiger Woods is a putting speed merchant. His controlled aggression with the putter is a sign of true confidence in his own game.

Wrapping them in from three feet is akin to a fine hip-flask slurp on a frost-white morning. Knocking putts in from 15 feet is even better – and if the occasional long one drops, jackpot! No wonder players on show pump the fist. The odds on it occurring in the first place may seem pretty slim, but if you can slide a couple of hefty big ones into the round for eagle or birdie, life just gets richer...

Improve your touch

The furthest from the hole we will probably ever have to putt (on the green) will be 60 feet. St Andrews, our Celtic homeland of the game with its huge double greens, might throw something a bit longer at us, but most courses won't. As I've said earlier, it's not much use driving the ball halfway to Africa, if our touch on the greens is reminiscent of a baby elephant in a hurry for lunch.

The hole is big

Half the battle is convincing our grey matter that the four-and-a-quarter-inch hole will accept the ball and not act like a trampoline. A hole is as wide as the top end on a pint glass (which should strike a chord with most taste buds). That all-time great champion and party animal Sam Snead loved to have a good time, and liked his friends to have an even better time, too. So, during one of his tournaments at his homeland palace of the Greenbrier in West Virginia, he made all the holes five inches wide. Rapture and joy! Putt after putt leap-frogged into darkness and birdie after birdie was notched – an inspired way to win friends!

The hole is 4.25 inches wide. The ball is 1.68 inches in diameter. It WILL go in!

Speed merchant

It is easy to get caught up in the technical side of putting and to forget that judging how hard you hit a putt is vital.

R U a glider or a rapper?

Find out which character of putting roll you are more comfortable with – and stick with it. If you like to see the ball leap into the hole and rattle the far side of the cup on short putts, then gliding the ball to its final breath as it 'dies' into the hole will not be your everyday method. Some people are better at one than the other; some can mix the two depending on green and weather conditions. If you're aware that you have two options, you can use them to your advantage.

Above: 'I have no breath...'

R U a beaurocrat or a broker?

In proper golf terms, they are known as: 'the lag' and 'the charge'.
A lag is when the ball dies – as if it can no longer bear to go on any longer. 'Golf is just too much' and, with a final gasp, the ball expires into the hole. The upside is that the hole seems bigger, the ball can slide into it from all sides and even rear entry is possible. However, on the downside, if you leave it short, it will never go in.
The charge is bayonet thrusting, kilts flying, nostrils flared... but charging is not just pure aggression. Controlled impetus dilutes the effects of the slope, and any bobbly bits on the green (spike marks, old pitch marks, tining slits) have little impact on the roll of the ball as it glides over the surface. This is the equivalent of driving along in the car when a series of 'traffic calming' humps pops up. Foot welded to the accelerator, you fly the bumps, then visit the garage for a new suspension.

The upside is that travelling at speed, the ball holds its line and any indentations in the green or spike marks will be of little significance. Controlled aggression also helps accelerate the putter head through impact.

However, if you don't get exactly the right line, the hole will bounce the ball off – there's no 'backdoor' sneaky here. On fast greens, this approach is brave indeed, and a clutch of three putts is more likely.

Personalize your golf ball

Carry an indelible marker pen in your golf bag and, before play, scribble a personal mark on the ball. It can be your initials, three dots, an arrow, or whatever you choose.

This is also useful when lining up the ball to putt. Having marked the ball, replace it with your personal identification facing the direction in which you wish to putt. (If you don't put a mark, then place the make of the ball towards the hole.)

Outside putting, marking the ball really is a good idea when you're searching for it in the 'bundi' – then you'll be absolutely sure that the ball you dug out of the undergrowth is yours. It is also a requirement when you're playing in competitions at County or higher level.

Left: Nice and easy...
David Duval exudes
complete self-control
at the Open.

Create a pre-shot routine

The pre-shot routine (PSR) should be an integral part of every single shot we play, from drives through to putts. Some top players cannot consider hitting their shots if any part of their PSR has been disturbed. They back off the ball and start all over again. For Scratch and Pro players, it is a subconscious habit.

Developing a controlled set routine for approaching every putt helps form a comfort zone so that, once all the data has been absorbed, we click into the 'wiggle twice, hands press forward' routine which triggers the takeaway – and we're off. Comfort zone equals confidence, and thus rate of success. We want that. Brief yourself to make your PSR second nature – the same way as teeth brushing at bedtime – and stick to this routine.

How to control your PSR

Remove any distractions and focus on your goal – sinking the putt. The key to success is repetition – just do the same thing every time. Familiarity counts. For five seconds, stare hard at the chosen line, then stare top-back of the ball. Forget all the mechanical parts – just feel where that hole is. Try and do the same things every time you putt. If you have one swish at the ball, do that. If you look at the hole three times and wiggle your toes, do that.

Trigger happy

Not everyone has a trigger, but many golfers do. Some are unaware they do anything at all. Once settled over the ball, satisfied the putt is 'lined-up' and pace decided, we do something

that triggers the take-away. For some, it could be a forward press of the hands, for others a squeeze of the toes. It can be the final placing of one finger on the shaft, or a deep breath. Whatever it is, there will be a mannerism that starts the action! It signifies to the brain that the pre-shot routine is completed and putting is about to commence.

Develop your own trigger. But don't get so obsessed with it that you cannot take the club back without being conscious of having done the action.

Above: **Weigh up the shot first. Even on the simplest of shots, don't forget your pre-shot routine.**

Above: **Trigger: 'and she's under starter's orders, and she's off'.**

Review and improve your putting portfolio

To do this, you need to take a detailed look at the three lengths of putt (short, medium and long); examine how you handle slopes, types of grass, climate, course familiarity, visualization and other sight issues.

Short, medium and long putts should always be approached differently. They each require individual parts of our putting expertise. For example, long putts ask us whether we are any good at judging distance; they are all about feel. Short putts are more about finding the right line and making a 'good stroke' – and if both those elements are correct, then the pace flows naturally, and the ball goes into the hole (we hope).

Again, some players, particularly those in the Hacker and, to a lesser extent, Club brackets, may grasp one length of putt better than another. There is nothing odd about this; people are just different. Also, sometimes we lose our touch with the shorts, mediums or longs for no apparent reason, and that can be desperately frustrating. By going through the following putting check-lists, we can not only calibrate differences but also, with luck, find an answer when things go wrong.

Hole language

Faced with short putts, most of us will just draw an imaginary line between our ball and the hole. Instead, pick a specific spot in or around the hole and focus on that. This is hole language: 'x' inches outside left. For example: 'I reckon that looks to be three

Left: **Zone in on detail. This makes the hole look as big as a bucket.**

inches outside the left lip' *or* 'x' inches outside left *or* inside left *or* middle *or* inside right *or* outside right. When playing foursomes, you can involve your partner in the green scene play. 'Just inside the right?' sounds as though you mean business.

Focus on one part of the hole

Shorts: 5–10 feet in

The 5-footers can cause knee knocking, even in golfers with titanium-lined guts. These are the real pressure putts. When the crunch comes, the muscles tense in anticipation, the heart beats faster and the eyeballs dry up. So during practice, like a golf commentator silently running through the opening sequence before going live, we must pretend to be in the furnace with the devil's henchmen gathering to drag us into oblivion if we miss.

Keeping it simple

A really short putt is under 2 feet long; the average player expects to hole these. Three feet can get the nerves jangling and 4-footers make the brain work very hard. Moreover, 6, 7, 8 and 10 feet become increasingly problematical. Some players take a couple of practice strokes to ease the worry. On very short putts (under 3 feet), when you know the line and feel confident, just settle over the ball and stroke it in. Make sure of the line (usually dead straight for 2 feet). Check the putter's head is square to the line and strike the putt firmly – don't hold back.

Shorts checklist

- If longer than 3 feet, bend down behind the ball to see the line.
- Pick your aim: e.g. the left edge of the hole.
- Free the tension – if it helps you.
- Stare at a chosen point in or around the hole.
- Draw an imaginary line between the ball and the exact point in the hole into which it will drop. Do this several times.
- Think 'Tick-Tock' smooth.
- Stay down over the putt until you hear the ball drop in the cup.

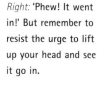

Right: 'Phew! It went in!' But remember to resist the urge to lift up your head and see it go in.

Left: Jose Maria Olazabal
of Spain is the matador
of sinking short putts.

Right: Do the 'Tiger Tunnel'. By making a narrow area of visual focus, you can black out distractions.

Mediums: 10–20 feet in

These are the length of your average car or Michael Jordan lying down and stretching e-v-erything. These beauties make a low score. Sinking these gives putting the Rock n'Roll adrenalin rush. Think of them as your chance to go one up on the course. If one drops, then another can too, and another.

Increase your success percentage

Depending on your standard of play, the Scratch player will expect to hole a fair percentage of these, whereas the Hacker is hugely relieved to get the ball close to the cup. As you walk onto the green, have a good look at the slopes around the putt. Bend down or bend over behind the putt to look at the line the ball will travel to the hole. Decide if the putt is straight, or breaking right to left or left to right. If in doubt or there's no obvious slope, aim straight...

Mediums checklist

● Walking on, look for general slopes around the line of putt.
● Bend down behind the ball to see the line.
● Pick a patch of grass to aim at and don't change your mind mid-flow.
● Have a couple of practice strokes to feel how hard to hit it and ease off the tension.
● Draw an imaginary line from your ball to the hole over your patch.
● Take a last look at your patch of grass and start staring at the ball.
● Think 'Tick-Tock' smooth.
● Trust your judgment and wait until the putt is nearly in the hole before you move up off the spot the ball left.

Longs: plus 20 feet in

Split the distance up. Walk to the halfway point between the ball and the hole. Let the putter hover over the surface but it must not touch the grass. Looking at the hole, make a couple of loose strokes and then walk back to the ball and feel what it would be like to double that distance. Look for the slopes and texture of the green. Walk up to and past the hole to judge the pace required. Assess how much to the left or right of the cup you will need to aim.

Ask for the pin to be attended if you cannot see 100 per cent. Judging the distance

Below: **Pick out a particular patch of grass on the line you have chosen and stick to what you have decided. Don't double guess yourself at the last minute.**

can be hard; asking for the pin to be held is not a sin and no-one will think you silly if you then sink the putt – even if it is only 15 foot long.

Having selected a specific patch of grass, take a couple of practice strokes to free up any stiffness and imagine how hard you are going to hit it. Have one last check on the patch of grass you are using to mark the direction, and then start looking at the ball – hard. Stare right into the ball and then don't look away until you have struck the putt.

Longs checklist

● Go for a prowl – up to the hole and past to judge the pace.

● Think how far left or right you need to aim.

● Pick a patch of grass and stick to your decision.

● Feel how hard to hit it – take a couple of practice strokes.

● Think 'Tick-Tock' smooth swing.

● Do a final check on aim – look at the grass.

● Stare at the ball and don't look up until you've hit it.

Right: **Think of being symmetrical: swing as far through as you swing back. This will encourage a good roll.**

Pace is more important than line

Slopes

There are uphill, downhill and, nastiest of all, side-sloping putts to test us. These putts are all on one level of green, whereas the tiered green (normally only with two distinct levels), could create total putting mayhem. Finally, in this section, putting off aprons is mentioned (as a welcome relief).

As a very general rule, allow twice the break you think there is on a putt. We amateurs tend to underborrow on most putts. This is why, when we miss the hole, it is usually on the 'low side' – known as the amateur side. If the ball is running out of puff and we have underborrowed, then it will tail off below the hole, with no hope of dropping in. If, however, the ball is dying but on the 'high side', like most pro putts, there is a chance that it can topple into the hole. The most dangerous of all is the side-on downhill putt. Try and float the ball in gently from the high side – the higher side of the cup. Aim to miss on the high side.

Downhill – speed merchant

A common misconception is that downhill putts are more difficult than uphill. They might be more dangerous and more sensitive to the line, but they are not necessarily more difficult. The emphasis of line and pace is different for each type of putt. As long as the ball is stroked carefully on line downhill, gravity keeps it online. Going uphill, the ball will waver off line if there is not sufficient pace. Some important downhill swing thoughts:

- Pick your line.
- Slow and smooth stroke.

Toe-it

On glisteningly fast greens, you can take some of the force out of the putter head by striking the putt with the toe of the club. This deadens the impact and means you can take a full slow stroke without the terror of ending up in the bunker the other side of the pin.

Left: **Some downhill putts do the runaway train thing when nearing the hole – the ball speeds up and races past, leaving you with a nasty five-footer to save par, bogey or even worse.**

35

Side slope

There is always one side of the slope you feel more comfortable with – it could be the break from right to left or left to right. To find out, test it out on the practice green. If the green is too flat, find a severe slope on the course.

On a 15-foot putt, the ball will gently curve off the slope towards the hole. (Obviously this depends on the steepness of the slope curve.) To make this happen you need to pick the spot on the green where you reckon the ball will decide to turn for home.

It helps to try and draw the curving line the ball will take in your mind's eye. Hold this imaginary line in your head and draw it again as you look at your chosen spot, then putt.

- Pick a spot where you think the putt will break.
- Line up to that spot.
- Imagine the curve.
- Strike the ball there – and trust yourself.

Uphill – crampon climber

Think 'slow green' and treat uphill putts in the same way. Judgement is vital here and when it gets to the point where you, the ball, the caddie and anyone else on the green is sliding backwards into the jaws of Arnie the Alligator, it could be designated a very steep slope.

- Try to get the ball a foot or two past the hole.
- Line is less important, unless there's a big break.
- Don't be afraid to give the ball a solid rap.

Tiers and aprons

More complex than simple uphill or downhill shots, tiers and aprons are the cuffs and collars of putting.

Uphill tiered greens (cuffs)

On a two-tiered green (like a golf cap: flat peak, flat top; nightmare slope in between), there is a tendency to leave the ball short, going uphill. Walk up to the hole and round the far side, looking back down the slope – all the time thinking how hard to hit it to get over the big ridge.

The ball should run over the crest, ready to die just around the hole. If the first putt fails to climb the hill, the second is generally struck far too quickly, without us gathering our thoughts again – so that fails as well. The third try may succeed but go way past the hole leaving a snaky downhiller. Hit it 50 per cent harder uphill than you first think.

Downhill tiered greens

The ball should just have enough puff to reach the cusp of the slope and then trundle on down towards the hole. Treat the putt as two halves. The first part is, hopefully, not hard, mostly flat and straight. Estimate how hard to hit it to reach the edge of the 'cliff'. Next comes judgement of the down slope. Always try and use the slope. There is a tendency to underborrow so aim off more than you think.

Whack it into the back of the cup

Aprons (collars)

These are more complex than simple uphill and downhill putting. Often it is better to putt than to attempt a tiny chip. For Hacker and, to some extent, Club, this is definitely true. If you are a yard off the green and the ground is fairly flat in front, there's nothing to stop the putter working well.

Above: Treat the shot as a long putt and hit it a bit harder to get over fringe grass. Using the putter from way off the green with a hump to go over can work well, too. The ball will jump into the air a bit, but you'll probably get closer like that than trying to construct a perfect little chip shot.

An OK putt = a good chip

Market research

Let's look at the effect of course familiarity on our putting. Along with this, climatic conditions and types of grass can throw a spanner in it, if we're not ready to react accordingly.

Playing at home or away?

Putting is one of the elements within golf that can result in a trip to the clinic. A cross between dread and misery are the emotions experienced when we have absolutely no idea what we are doing on the greens. Try to use your home course knowledge when playing a strange venue. Say you are faced with a steep downhill putt of 25 feet and are terrified of running through into the bunker at the back. Your home course 7th hole has a similar green. Use your home course knowledge to reassure your confidence levels.

The green scene

These are generalizations but they may help you get in the right frame of mind.
● Winter inland course = lush and slow = less roll on the ball, harder hits from a heavier putter will keep the ball on line.
● Winter links course = medium to fast = rolling well, good for smooth stroking.
● Summer inland course = quicker, but still can be lush. Pace is dependent on weather variables. Can be surprisingly slow due to greenkeepers letting the grass grow for that 'one important tournament in July'.
● Summer links course = super fast = big time wind affected, 10 foot in: straight back

Grain

When on tough, coarse Bermuda grass, look for the grain. Grain affects the *speed* of the putt.
● Shiny green grass means putting with the grain = faster.
● Dull green grass means putting against the grain = slower.
Grain affects the *break* of the putt (the twist, the wiggle, the involuntary slither).
● There's less break when you're putting against the grain.
● There's more break when you're putting with the grain.
To read the grain, do the following:
1 Look at the cup. The side of it will show you which way the grass leans. If the right side of the cup is jagged, the grain is growing from right to left.
2 Look at the cup. Does it have jagged edges? Affirmative, and you've got a slow green.
3 Look at the cup. Does it have razor-sharp edges? If so, your green is quick, quick, quick.

and straight through, get it rolling and let it go. Out comes the light-weighted putter.

In spring and autumn, when the frost breaks or with twigs on the greens, it is even more of a task to get the ball into the hole. Do a spot of gardening before you putt; remove impediments but don't be pernickety about it – sweeping that last grain of sand or blade of grass probably won't make as much difference to the ball as you think it will. Balls are remarkably resilient when it comes to staying on line – on medium to slow greens. Fast greens are another story.

Investigations and audits

Treat every golf course as unique. It is dangerous to assume that all greens behave in a similar fashion. Pace can vary from morning to afternoon, day to day, and sometimes even between greens. Dew slows them up; wind and sun make them speedier.

It is competition day on a strange course. How can you get a feel for these alien greens? Don't trust the practice green. Instead, get out there and test the greens (if allowed) before the round. Try out some long ones and, if you feel conspicuous aiming at the flag, just putt from one side of the green to the other. If it's a strokeplay tournament, the rules say you can't putt on the greens (or play on any part of the course) on the day of play prior to starting your round – you are testing the surface. In matchplay, you can. If there's a practice round to be had, take advantage of it.

Ask around

Testing the actual green surface is not always practical or advisable when entering the monthly medal as it smacks of too much keenness. Instead, hit a few putts on the practice green and then stare at one of the real greens to see if it has long grass, looks bald or dried up. Ask around: try the members and the staff in the pro shop.

Above: We can learn quite a bit from our playing partners or our opponents by observing how their putts behave – just like life through a lens.

Left: Samuel L Jackson leaves Hollywood behind for blustery St Andrews to check out the greens. Treat every golf course as unique.

Personal quirks

They say every human is genetically unique (98 per cent or so). This is also the case with putting DNA. However, a conventional, simple set up and stroke is easier to fix when it goes wrong. Odd styles, weird tempos and bizarre swings just make Doctor Diagnostic's task trickier to analyse and treat.

Putting stroke fluidity

Unlike Pinocchio, we do not want to appear stiff. Fluidity really only comes with familiarity with the putter. Short of being born with one in the paw, there is no other option but to spend some 'quality time' getting to know your newest best friend – your putter. Most of us are confined to indoor life, Monday to Friday 8 am to 7 pm. Office putting practice can help solve business dilemmas, stimulate thought processes and can motivate those creative juices for that new ad campaign.

Feel – low back, hit and up

Take the club head back low to the ground, strike the putt and then keep the momentum going by following through upwards – rather than following through low to the ground.

Right: Sam Torrance in action with his legendary long-shafted putter. Use the style that suits you – but get to know your putter well.

Do your own thing – but the stroke is 'back and thru'

See your line

Think of gymnasts performing on the bar. Their balance on such a thin, narrow strip of wood is amazing. How do they stay on it when they cartwheel, jack-knife and somersault in the air and then land perfectly on nothing wider than a slither of A4 paper? They visualize that their landing zone is the width of a surf-board.

Good putting depends on being able to visualize the ball travelling along an imaginary line towards and into the hole. Hacker's and Club's most common fault is to address the ball with the face of the putter *open*. So always check the club face is square to the line of the hole.

Grip the club for a putt, line yourself up and then take your right hand off the club and, being careful not to alter the club face, stand behind the putt and look to see if the putter face is at right angles to the hole. You'll be surprised just how often you are aiming just a touch right.

Mirror check

To check that you are standing square to the ball, set up for a putt in front of a full-length mirror. Practise some swings in front of it and see if your feet, hips, hands and shoulders are all square to the line of the mirror.

- Stand square.
- Keep your head still.

Dodgy eyes

Some days putts roll in and we can see the line blindfolded. Other days it could be chalked out on the green but we can't see it. Our eyes just cannot find the right line to hit along. Eyesight and feel are the two most important elements to putting. Several top money earners have resorted to the laser to improve their vision, Laura Davies and Tiger being just a couple of them. What you might read as straight may be offset due to astigmatism or a change in your eyesight, so get your eyes checked.

Left: **You can check whether you are square to the ball by setting up in front of a full-length mirror. As you swing, check that your feet, hips, hands and shoulders are square to the line of the mirror.**

Putting practice drills

It is always worth investing in our putting. It will never be really good enough unless we work at it. The one element which is integral to successful putting is self-confidence. Here are 12 drills to try.

Distance judgement drill

This routine helps speed control and fine-tunes distance judgement for short to medium putts.

- Take five tees.
- Starting five feet away from you, put a tee down in the green.
- In a diagonal line, every two feet after that, put another tee down.
- With five balls, putt from the same spot to each tee.
- Each ball should give up its last breath on arrival at the tee.

Right: **In the distance judgement drill, you putt from the same spot to five different tees in the green.**

Far right: **Use a coin to make the target zone smaller, and then putt to it. Practise this drill with various distances.**

Target lock-on drill

This focuses the eyes on a smaller target and hones precision. To make the target zone smaller:

- Instead of a hole, use a coin.
- Putt to it.
- The distance can be anything from a few to 15 feet or so – it's up to you.

Clock drill

By changing the angle of attack, yet keeping the same distance, concentration is improved while building a repetitive action.

● Take three balls (that's really the comfortable number that will fit into the hole at once, and, as they're all going to rattle in, that's ideal).

● Work from midnight clockwise all through the day and night.

● Hole three balls on each hour. If time slips by (you miss a putt), it's turn the clock back and start again.

Above: Imagine a clock face around the hole and work on holing the three balls from the different hour positions on the clock.

Midnight munchies drill

This a positive thought-builder. Again, with three balls, and the clock...

● This time only putt at midnight, 3, 6 and 9 pm.

● Sink every one from three feet and then work outwards to six and nine feet.

● By that time it'll be dark and, if you're anything like me, you'll have backache and need a cup of Earl Grey.

Tramliner drill

Keeping the toe and heel of the putter from crashing into the tees reaffirms that you are swinging the club face on line.

● Take eight tees.

● Stick them in the ground a couple of inches apart like tramlines, so that the putter head just fits inside them.

● The idea is to go straight back and straight through without touching these tees with either the heel or toe of the putter.

Left: **Practise swinging the putter head back and through the two rows of tees without touching them.**

Railway block drill

Like the tramlines drill, this checks that you are keeping the putting stroke simple and helps muscle memory.

● Place a driver parallel to the hole on the ground.

● Keeping the putter head at 90 degrees, swing back and forwards to the hole, always with the toe of the putter up against the shaft – at least until after impact.

Fringe fondling drill

This helps judgement. Imagine you are on a bowling green and roll that ball.

● Forget the hole.

● Find a space about 30 feet long and flat on the putting green.

● With six balls, putt towards the fringe (or apron, or edge of the green – whatever you know it as).

● This can be varied with uphill, downhill and side-winders after the straightforward option has been mastered, or until someone else crowds your space.

Above: Putting towards the fringe on different greens will help improve your judgement.

Above: This simple drill helps build muscle memory. All you do is to swing back and forth to the hole, keeping the putter head at 90 degrees to the shaft of the driver lying on the ground.

Corridor creeper drill

Judgment of distance (translating what is in our head to our hands) is vital in a long putt. Speed control is the goal. This exercise is great when it's pouring llamas and hippos outside.

● Find a long (30 foot plus) corridor with a reasonable carpet (not one that is so bare the ball won't stay still) and a wall at the end.

● Take some balls and putt towards the wall.

● The idea is to make the ball just touch the wall.

Chunky Monkey Drill

By splitting up a long distance into smaller sections, our brain can handle the problem easier. Next time you're faced with a huge putt, you can mentally split it into two or three pieces. This is one way to aid distance judgment.

● Stick half a dozen balls down on the putting surface, on the line of a long putt, at 5-foot intervals.

● Divide the monster into chunks.

● Starting with the closest to the hole, sink one by one, working back to that eagle putt.

The Ernie drill

Ernie 'The Big Easy' Els uses this one to make sure his body doesn't move over short putts. It is really difficult to over-move without a backswing. This makes sure that the hands lead the club head.

● Stand over the ball on a six footer and putt it – without a backswing.

● Push the ball towards the target.

● In hockey, when taking a penalty 'put in' you push the ball with the stick – no backswing. Same thing.

Below: **This drill helps you to practise pushing the ball towards the hole, making your hands lead the club head. There should be no backswing.**

Above: **Work your way along the line of balls, putting them one at a time into the hole.**

Putting warm-ups

In an ideal world, when we all have more than one minute to put our shoes on and run to the first tee, these warm-up drills pull the eye-hand coordination away from driving up the motorway at 90 mph (late again!), and towards golf.

Speed read warm-up

1 Putt 3 balls *uphill* 5 times from 20–30 feet.
2 Put a tee in the ground to mark the spot you putted from. Don't focus on getting them in – just memorize how hard you hit it.
3 Now putt *downhill* with the same strike, starting from the hole to the tee.
4 Look how far past the tee the ball runs.
5 Do this from 10–15 feet then from 5 feet.

Breakers warm-up

With 3 balls, from 4, 8, and 15 feet from the hole:
● See how the ball reacts to the break.
● Find a left to right, and right to left slope.

Die, glide and rap warm-up

With 3 balls, four feet from the hole:
● Ball 1: Get it to just dribble into the cup (die).
● Ball 2: Get it to glide into the cup (glide).
● Ball 3: Get it to ram into the back of the cup and jump about (rap).

Regular warm-up

Some players love practising for hours on golf's 'dough' end; others get backache after 20 minutes. Usually there is barely enough time to tap in half a dozen putts before teeing off the first. A regular putting warm up is unrealistic, so try the following instead.

Long and short warm-ups

Watch the speed on the long ones, and wait for the 'plop' in the hole on the short ones. With two balls:
For rhythm and pace: hit a handful of 10–20 footers.
For distance: hit a couple of really long ones.
For confidence and focusing the eye: hit a handful of 4–5 footers and a couple of tiddlers.

The rushed warm-up

And if you are really pushed for time, try this.
Beside the first tee: this is all about re-focusing the eyes and calming the mental rush down to a suitable state so that the front nine holes are not a putting wasteland.
● Drop the ball you are playing with and stare really hard at it on the ground for 30 seconds.
● Hold the putter and do a few pendulum swings with no ball.
On the first green: don't be ambitious early on in the round by rapping long putts past the hole and then putting pressure on the tricky six-foot putt back. If there is time after you have completed the first or second hole, do the following:
● Drop your ball down on the green.
● Glide a few mid-range putts in order to test the pace.

Left: 'You know, Nick, I think that we've been out here practising for hours...' Colin Montgomerie and Nick Faldo working on their short putts.

Handling a recession

This section is devoted to troubleshooting: remedies for regular problems that most of us encounter at some time in our golfing careers. All golfers have gone through this and much worse and will go through it again. That's golf for you.

Four-foot nightmares

Everyone has a particular length they detest or fear. Four feet are the nastiest. Ninety-nine per cent of the time there is little break, so make sure the putter head is square to the line, and give it a positive wrap.

Practise with your eyes shut

Spend a bit longer than you usually would lining up and settling over the ball, then shut the eyes and 'feel' the way to the hole. You'll be surprised how many go in. When you return to the sighted challenge you'll have that added confidence that 'I can sink these even with my eyes shut'.

Shortfall

Always putting short of the hole is one of the commonest amateur traits. According to Dave Peltz, the ex-NASA scientist shortgame guru, the ball needs to travel 17 inches past the hole to be at the best speed to drop into it.

● Place a club on the ground a foot or so behind the hole and use a handful of balls.

● Stand about 15 or more feet from the hole.

● Putt to the hole but aim to make the ball just run out of steam as it touches the club's shaft. The sight and feel of the ball rolling past the hole and gently stopping will imprint in the subconscious, and the next time a mid to long putt pops up, the ball will not be left short.

Right: **If you have a tendency to putt short of the hole, place a club on the ground behind it and practise putting to the club shaft so that the ball runs past the hole.**

Missing left, missing right

It is demoralizing when on short putts (under 10 feet) there is no consistency to missing. Whether the ball is 'pushed' right or 'pulled' left makes no difference. We need to check the line of our stroke is on line to the hole.

Take some advice from Nick Faldo. He checks his line by placing a club on the ground parallel to the hole. You check your stroke by running the putter head back and forth on top of the shaft. He maintains that a good stroke is one that moves back slightly inside the shaft and then straight through to the target – 'chasing the line'.

Also, check the putter head is square to the hole. To help with this, do the Railway block (page 44). Now check your alignment: is the club face really square? Remember to keep the putting stroke simple: back low, hit through and up.

Meltdown: the Yips

This is one of golf's cruel diseases, a virus seeping through the game. It's no use if everywhere off the green we are indestructible; if the Yips take hold, then you will be utterly miserable. The worry of not being able to putt infects its way back to the tee shots like snake bite poison up your limbs.

The Yips are an inability to perform the smooth action required to stroke the ball towards the hole. They are the golfing physical equivalent of someone with a violent twitch.

Yips can be cured (phew!)

There are four main ways to conquer the Yips.

1 Face them

Face the problem straight on and talk to yourself – hard. Refuse to accept the Yips. Remain glued to the putting green until you hit so many putts without a twitch that the Yip memory fades like fax paper print.

2 Forget the hole

While you try to figure out where it all went wrong, don't putt to a hole. This takes the pressure off and re-focuses the mind on the mechanics of the putting stroke. Instead, focus on making a 22-carat stroke – to anywhere on the green other than the hole.

3 Alter something

Take your mind off the problem by trying one of the following. Get yourself a new putter. Alternatively, try out a new grip or a different stance. You could even experiment with a change in tempo.

4 Change your attitude

Golf is an emotional experience and if Yips turn up, degrees of fear, loathing and panic (followed by a resigned helpless shoulder slump) set in. After a few Yippy rounds we expect the worst, but this can be turned around. Just think of a place you feel really happy in and smile (even if it's the last thing you feel like trying). Stay in your happy place and putt.

Above: **Sack the Yips, and relocate to your Happy Face.**

Remember: never up – never in

Summary

There is a set routine to putting (and most shots), much like withdrawing money from your ATM cashpoint machine (remember: sinking putts = making 'money').

Choose service

Short, medium or long. Slow or fast. Uphill, side or downhill. Find the line. Scout that putt out.

Punch in your PIN

Birdie or safety putt. Lag or charge putt. You choose.

Check credit balance

Feel the pace, check your line – it's dress rehearsal time.

Select cash

Settle over the ball. Final checks – PSR (Pre-Shot Routine) moment.

Take card back and remove cash

Trigger the takeaway, pendulum back and through stroke. Lead with your hands.

CHAPTER THREE

Chips and lobs

Think of chips as crisps. They possess that sensory pleasure known as 'the crunch'. Golfing chips, those delicate shots, will not perform without having an impact crunch. This does not mean that the ball is hit hard, just crisply. Thus the frustrating 'flubbed' shot, where the hands appear to die right on impact as the club head gets ahead of them, can be prevented.

Chips or pitches?

The next two chapters split shots from 100 yards to the hole by distance from the hole. We amateurs are not always sure of the difference between a chip and a pitch shot so let's take a look at what these terms mean.

Little shots

These are 10–20 feet from the edge of the putting surface (or within 20 yards of the pin):

Chip: A low running shot made from just off the green (probably no further out than 10 feet from the edge of the putting surface).

Lob: A small pitch, an intimate shot. This is used when there is an obstacle in between you and the pin. Probably no further out than 20 feet from the edge of the green.

Bigger shots

These shots are 30–100 yards from the pin:

Pitch: A higher trajectory shot made from further out – from 20 up to 100 yards from the pin.

Punch: This is a larger shot, which is used often in windy conditions. The benefit is that the lower trajectory keeps the ball on line and it should stop fairly quickly with spin. These are from 30–100 yards out.

All these shots can be played with a variety of clubs. What we amateurs are poor at understanding is that playing a less impressive style of shot is often the safest way to get the ball beside the hole on a regular basis – so we score better, have more confidence, take the pressure off the long game, and don't end up hating golf.

Right: Philip Rowe of Great Britain and Ireland chips to perfection during the 1999 Walker Cup at Nairn Golf Club in Scotland.

Creating that crisp chip

We will now step into the culinary world. Life often provokes minor upsets which can be assuaged with comfort food or a meal out (edible retail therapy). We would all agree that we benefit physically and mentally from the concept of nourishment. So does our golf.

Golf has its small upsets – we come up short of the flag, we pepper greens outside left or right. A nasty taste in our mouths develops when we can't control our chipping. Good chipping brings spice back into the game.

Tasty chips – saving shots

If our 6, 7 and 8 irons to the green fly tangentially like Scud missiles on abort, the day can still be saved with brilliant chipping. Even if life isn't quite that drastic, but our golfing taste buds aren't functioning on full alert, the inner glow that pulses 'we know how to get up and down' enables us to avoid 'golfer's indigestion'.

Final scores for the hole are relative. Hacker would be engagement announcement happy and Club would be highly contented if a bogey 5 was salvaged when there was no chance of landing on the green for three on a par 4. Pro will expect a birdie, and hope for an eagle, having almost driven the green.

Get rid of the stiff set-up

Newcomers to chipping, or players with no confidence in their ability around the green, exhibit *rigor mortis* in their upper body. Their set-up is stiff and their swing stilted. They often jump stiffly back and up off their stance immediately after hitting the shot, emitting an anxious: 'Stop, I didn't mean it, I'm sorry!', and the ball dives for cover over the far side of the green into a lake.

Learning how the chip shot works and where the ball is meant to land, bounce and roll is the Starter; being able to execute it efficiently is the Main Course. Depending on your ability, certain types of chip may be better left in the larder. For Hacker (who may be happy to climb no further up the golfing ladder), it is enough to master one shot with two different clubs:

- A 7 or 8 iron
- A wedge.

Good chipping gives you confidence

Chip basics

It is fine to have some personal preferences about equipment for chipping. For a flat run in to the flag, if you are happier using a 7 iron rather than an 8, then use the 7. If you need to feel comfortable by taking three 'swishes' at the grass before you tackle the shot – do it.

Basic chip grip

Aim for minimal hand action. Tiger Woods uses his putting grip. If you are starting the game, then his example must be right. For us old hands, it may be too late to change from using the full swing grip.

Basic chip set up

Whatever quirks you may or may not cultivate, this is the method that most of us should opt for:

● Putting or full swing grip – normal is OK but putting gives more feel.

● Grip down the shaft for extra control and feel.

● Elbows soft against your sides – encourages a relaxed, free swing.

● Set the body open to target (left foot back a bit) to release the club face to the hole.

● Narrow stance (about a foot wide) – brings the body closer to the ball, making the shoulder tilt easier.

● Ball mid stance opposite left ankle – pushes hands forwards, aiding a crisp strike.

● Hands pushed forwards helps downward impact.

● 80 per cent of weight on your left leg avoids the club overtaking the hands and deceleration.

● Knees flexed – good for rhythm and stops stiffness.

Above: **When chipping, you should always keep your hand action minimal. Although you can use your full swing grip, you may find a putting grip preferable.**

Chip swing

● Zone in on the top half of the body; keep the bottom half quiet.

● Think chain-reaction – shoulders/arms/hands (move the shoulders first; the rest will follow).

● Hinge the wrists – only a bit – and be sure to keep the left wrist solid and stiff.

● Body does a tiny 'tick-tock' motion.

● Think *crisp* strike (imagine the club face munching a bite out of the turf).

● Finish the swing – lead with the back of the left hand to the target.

Above and right: **Smack that ball... and don't forget to accelerate through impact.**

The mantra: 'Accelerate through impact'
'Accelerate through impact'
'Accelerate through impact'

Where to land on the green

Aim for a flat part of the green. Failing that, try to go for a dip rather than a mound. Landing on a hump will turn the heat up on the unpredictable bounce of the ball. A dip or an indentation will remove some of the loft from the shot and shoot the ball forwards – so be sure to allow for that.

Wrist break!

The most vital point to remember when chipping is: very little *wrist break*. Keep the 'back and through' action as simple as you can, without breaking the wrists much. This controls the distance that the ball runs. You can control all the movement by the tick-tocking of your shoulders.

● Keep the left wrist firm and flat.
● The back of the left hand leads to the target.

Above: **Try to keep the left wrist firm and flat. The back of the left hand should lead towards the target.**

Left: **Try putting a biro, emery board or ice-lolly stick under your watch strap on the back of your left hand – that will keep it stiff. (A tip from Senior US Tour Pro Gary 'Mad Walrus moustache' McCord.)**

Chip varieties

Just when you thought you'd mastered the basic chip, up comes a variable that throws panic on the walk up to the green. Here are five situations, all of which require greater or lesser differences in approach: Bump and run, Lob flip up, Putt-chip, Uphill v Downhill and Rough and hairy.

Visualizing the appropriate style of chip requires a touch of tangential meditation followed by competent application. Always reaching for the 52/55/56/60 degree wedge when really a 'down the shaft' 7 iron fits the bill is a fault belonging to most of us. Pros have developed an innate ability to know which shot best suits the situation; but even they can get carried away with the Lob Wedge Wonder. Trying to get 'too cute' with the shot by always opting for the Lob will mean a much less proficient player may beat them to the pin with their sensible low running chip. So here are a few pointers that enable us to move the ball close to the hole without serving up the same concoction to the same guests, time and again, and again, and again, and again.

Bump and run

This shot is useful on approaches from near the green (up to about 30 feet out), where there are no bunkers or dips in between the ball and the target. The whole point of the bump and run shot is to start the ball off low so that it hits the deck with its caterpillar legs running at Mach 1 towards the hole until it has no breath left, gracefully expiring 18 inches from the pin. What's the advantage? The less time spent in the air, the more likely the ball is to keep out of trouble.

When to play it

This shot is usually played on a links course. You need to be about 20 to 30 feet from the pin, with a flat run in to the flag.

See the shot in your head first

Club selection

Ideally, you should use a straighter-faced club, a 7 or an 8, rather than a wedge. However, if there is a faint glimmer of doubt in your confidence about using a 7 iron (gripping down a bit), then stick to a hands forward, de-lofted wedge off the back foot. You need to give yourself the best chance of 100 per cent confidence over how the ball will react when coming off the club face. Therefore, find your comfort club.

Set up

For the set up, go down the grip and adopt a narrow stance. Keeping your hands forward, move your weight mid-forward with the ball opposite your left heel.

How to play it

The club head should be low to the ground through the shot. Pick a flat spot for the ball to land on. You need a short, neat swing, and don't forget to look at the back of the ball.

Left: When playing the bump and run, set up with your hands down the grip and a narrow stance. Keep your swing short and hit through with the club head low to the ground.

Lob flip up

This is required in the following situation: ball –
bunker – not much green to work with – hole.
With this potentially embarrassing confrontation
in the future, write down 'serious help required'.
Short of bribing Mr Phil Mickelson, an expert at
this shot (with his lob wedge, he can stuff it up
your left nostril), with vast sums of 'wonga' to
play these shots for us, there must be a panic
button to stop the kettle boiling dry.

How to flip up

With either a wedge or, if there is enough
grass underneath the ball, a sand-iron, open
your feet (pull back the left foot and turn the
toes out towards the hole). Your knees will be
nearly at 90 degrees to your body and feel a
bit restricted. Open the club face, big time.
(Open it any more and you'll feel like you will
hit the ball out of the socket.) Then grip the
club – gently. Your arms should be nestling
down and feeling relaxed – you simply can't
manufacture this shot if they're all tense and
stretched out stiffly. Your knees should be
flexed and bouncy.

Remember, above all, that the ball position
is dead centre – not forward. If the ball is too
far forward in your stance, a miserly thin or

grotesque fat shot is in danger of appearing as the bottom arc of the swing is out of place. Positioning the ball back in the stance is good for de-lofting shots, but a ball that is too far forward is good for nothing.

When to play it

Play this shot when there is a bunker or hazard in between the ball and the pin. You should use either a wedge or sand wedge.

Set up

Open the stance way left (probably 10 plus feet left of the target). Your club face should be wide open. Grip the club easy and always remember to flex the knees.

How to play it

Take two to three practice backswings to feel how hard you will hit it. You need a U-bend shape swing. Use your wrists to set the club on the right path in the backswing. Swing along your foot line (out to in) and hold the club face open through impact and finish.

Below: **With the ball in the centre of your stance, swing out to in, holding the club face wide open as it comes through impact and at the finish. Don't forget to flex your knees.**

This shot is for the brave

Putt-chip

The putt-chip, chip-putt, putt-putt-chip, chip-putt-putt, putt-chip-putt, chip-putt-cpih, ptut –phci, chpi-ttup. Just pretend that you're aged seven and try saying, 'Red lorry, yellow lorry, red lorry, yellow lorry, red lorry, yellow lorry' – *fast*.

The putt-chip shot is required on those occasions when the ball lies no more than a couple of yards off the green; with no obstacles between it and the flag. Putt-chips remove any potential for wrist action

interference. By treating the swing (or movement as it's so little) as a putting action, the odds of the ball ending up somewhere near the pin, are increased.

Grip

You can use either your usual putting grip or your normal swing one. The advantage of the putting grip is that it deadens the hands and wrists and reminds the brain that this shot is an extension of a long putt.

When to play it

There should be no obstacles between the ball and the pin and a pretty flat run to the hole. Use a straight-edged iron, probably a 5, 6 or 7.

Set up

Go down the grip and use your putting grip – aiming for soft pressure, more feel. Think 'long putt' for swing. With your feet close together, open the stance a little. Your weight should favour your left side.

How to play it

Effectively, you are playing a long putt so you should treat this putt-chip shot in exactly the same way.

In order to deaden the strike, if you're using a wedge, you can tip the club face away from you (putting it on its toe at address). This not only helps deaden the strike but also the ball will be a bit more controllable and will still have sufficient loft to hop over any trouble.

Left: You should feel as though you are slightly tilting your wrists up and away to create that putting position. As you start to swing, think 'long putt'.

Think: bounce, bounce, bounce... roll

Uphill chip

This shot is required when the ball is close to the green with the hole higher than the ball. When travelling uphill the ball will check on its first bounce, more than expected. This takes the energy out of its roll forward. At the same time, if it is a steep climb up to the flag, you do not want to leave yourself a downhill putt on the way back.

When to play it

The uphill slope dictates you align your spine with the slope. Uphill, keep the weight moving up the hill after impact. Use an 8 or 9 iron, or 52 (Utility) wedge. You don't want too much loft, unless there is a hazard (bunker) between you and the hole.

Set up

Pick a spot to land on, a few feet further up on the green than if it were flat.

How to play it

Use the same stroke as described in chip basics (see page 55). Don't fall backwards – keep your weight towards the target.

Left: Align your spine with the uphill slope, keeping your weight moving up the hill after impact.

Downhill chip

This is required when the ball is close to the green with the hole lower than the ball. Let us assume that the green is fast. Our ball is lying just off it, on the apron, with an adequate lie (not buried in thick grass or on parched or bare turf). With 30 or so feet to go to the pin, and downhill, the bunker on the far side lures like the Black Hole. The safest thing is to use a wedge, as the club's loft will raise the ball over the rough ground and make it sit quietly on the green. If you are on a downhill lie, some loft will be removed from the wedge.

When to play it

The opposite of the uphill shot, the slope again dictates what you must do. A pitching wedge is the safest option.

Set up

Pick a spot to land on, a few feet nearer to you than for a flat chip.

How to play it

Use the basic chip stroke. The ball will keep rolling more than you expect, due to gravity. Stay still over the chip for a while longer.

Right: **After striking the ball, feel as though you've squeezed your hands together. This prevents a thinned scuttler dashing into the opposite bunker.**

Rough and hairy chip

This is required when the ball is skulking in long grass, heather or scrub near the green. Rough and hairy golf can even catch the Pro.

It is the 2001 Tournament Players Championship, Day 3 at Sawgrass, Florida. Scott 'Choke' Hoch (poor guy, nicknames always stick, especially when it's a short putt for the Masters) was embedded a yard from the green in jungle grass – so deep his shoes were invisible. He had to chop down on the ball, get it rolling and then stop it, all on a dime. Nightmare! Top guy looking perturbed big time. It would have been so easy to decelerate on impact and leave it buried, on the other hand there's no control and he could fly it right through. Scott got out of purgatory, but what would we amateurs do?

Above: If you are inches from the green but in thick rough, the longer and steep backswing should feel like a guillotine dropping gently on the ball's head – and the ball pops forward and rolls into the hole!

When to play it

When there is either long grass or thick heather surrounding the ball and it is tough to get close. Use a lofted lob or sand wedge.

Set up

Hold the club more firmly than usual, focusing on your left hand as the grass will turn it over. Put the ball back in the stance.

You need a very steep backswing to create the chopping action to get the ball flying out of the rough. Wrist break should be big.

How to play it

Use a longer swing than you think (the rough reduces the club head's effectiveness). Don't worry about following through too much. Chop and stay down.

Long grass means use a longer swing

Curing your faults

There are three flaws that can scupper good chip scrambling: thinning it; fluffing it; and digging divots. Since we all will experience these horrors, it is useful to be able to recognize why they happen and quickly rectify the situation.

Thinned shots

Two things cause thins: a floppy left wrist at impact; and jerking back up off the shot. Hitting off a bare bikini-waxed lie can spice things up, too. Club's and perhaps Match's left arm grinds to a halt right on impact. Meanwhile, the club head overtakes the hands in a nasty scooping action.

Salvage: Work on a positive finish position to stop the club head overtaking the hands. Do left-arm only chips with a pencil pushed inside your watch strap.

Fluffed shots

The culprit is deceleration of the club at impact (slowing down just as you come to hit the ball). Le Fluff is what I term the 'chicken' shot. It is a nervy twitch which, as you stand poised over the ball with a chip of 40 feet to the pin and people watching, your hands go deaf. The brain says 'weight on my forward leg, nice and smooth, keep my head down', the arms appear to go through the motions, but when the point of impact comes, the hands pull back.

Salvage: One way round this is to concentrate on a specific thought during the shot. Talk to yourself (quietly). The following may help:

● My hands must lead the club face.
● I must strike down and forwards towards the hole.

If the club is accelerated into the back of the ball crisply, it will pop forwards with a touch of spin.

Fat shots

Oversized divots are produced when the angle of attack is too steep. Have you had that 'I want to be an ostrich' experience? Imagine immaculately groomed fairways – the type Augusta National, shrine to The Masters, produces. So smooth. No blemishes. Perfect play area. Go near the greens and you are treading on pure satin. Sacred turf. Wielding your wedge, the club attacks the ball but desecrates top Augusta honcho Hootie Johnson's pride and joy by removing a sod the size of Manhattan, and the ball flies insolently a few yards. U R not a chopper!

Salvage: Check your ball position. Is it too far forward? It should be opposite your right ankle. Shift your weight – back on the right foot, through on the left a little – this stops the hands and wrists becoming too active.

Chipping with woods

Butch Harmon taught Tiger to do the Wood Chip. Nearly every one of us has since tried to copy him – and it's easy to master. Use a 3 wood. Play it only when the ball is lying well (up) on the fringe of the green or in light rough. It works because the wide base of the wood prevents the grass latching onto the club.

If you watch Tiger, you will see that he takes the club head away from the ball low, so it brushes the top of the grass. He uses his wrists to pop the club face into the back of the ball, keeping the back of his left hand moving down the target line.

When to play it

Play this shot when the ball is lying up in the rough on the fringe of the green. Use a 3, or something like it, wood.

Set up

Grip down the shaft to the steel part and make sure you stand really close to the ball.

How to play it

Always take the club head away low to the ground, brushing the grass. Use the wrists a bit. Make the back of the left hand lead the club to the hole.

Left: **Play this shot with a 3 wood if the ball is in light rough right on the fringe of the green. Make sure that you grip well down the shaft and take the club head away low to the ground.**

Techniques to master

Here are four drills for you to try; the first two help create a solid action whereas the next two are good when things go 'up the spout'.

Solidify your action

For this you will need the following: a spare practice green (or flat, mown lawn) and 20 or so *good* balls (there is no point in using cut or hacked-about ones as the strike and roll will not do you justice). For a general chipping club, try using the 8 iron.

How to play it

Keep the ball opposite the right ankle, feet close together. Think 'tick tock' back and forwards, and lead off with the shoulders. Focus on the left wrist remaining unbent. Pay attention to your action, not where the balls end up.

Muscle memory builder

For this drill you will need the following: a spare practice green (or flat area), 10 balls and a wedge (Utility best). Try to relax.

How to play it

Take the 10 balls and then hit them to various distances, ranging from 10–30 feet off the green. Try to focus on sensing what you feel in your arms and hands – the bigger the swing, the more lively the difference. Now take another tranche of balls and pretend each shot is to win a major competition. Hit them again to the same range of distances.

Right: **Eyes glued to the back of the ball... and to the blade of grass underneath it even after you've hit. It's the chipping action, not where the ball goes, that's important here.**

Ernie easy-over drill

This drill, which is named after Ernie Els, aims to help you develop a smooth chipping rhythm (less hands and wrists). You need a flat area, 10 balls and a chipper – choose whatever feels easy, such as a 9 iron.

How to play it

Start with both hands on the club, as usual. Take the right hand off and rest it on your right buttock. Using your body (keep your wrists and hands 'quiet'), swing back and through the small chipping movement.
Tip: Your left elbow should touch your gut throughout (keeps things connected).

Hands leading club face

For this drill, you need a flat area to land on, a large emery board, nail file or long biro/pencil and 10 balls. Club choice is yours (see page 57).

How to play it

Stick the emery board, nail file or pencil on the inside of your left wrist, tucking it under the watchstrap. This feels awkward but keeps the left-leading hand flat towards the target and stops the wrists getting over-involved on the backstroke and throughstroke. Feel how straight and solid your left wrist remains as you concentrate on 'finishing' the chip off, following through towards the target.

Left: Practise by focusing on leading with the back of the left hand while keeping the right hand free.

Summary

Compared to the hard slog of food shopping, preparation and cooking, chipping is the equivalent of boiling an egg, Delia-style.

Prepare

Ground layout – is it flat and how far to the pin? Pick the best chip landing spot and visualize the ball's journey to the hole. Select a club – anything from a 6 iron to a wedge – to get the ball rolling on the ground as soon as possible.

Cook

Use either a putting or full swing grip. Grip down the shaft. Narrow stance with ball mid to opposite left ankle. Lean towards target (slightly). Very little wrist action needed. Keep hands ahead of ball through a crisp impact strike.

Devour

Swing back and through for the best chips, keep your knees soft and look at the spot where the ball was nestling – after you've struck it.

CHAPTER FOUR

Pitches and punches

One of the most vital elements to good pitching is good rhythm. At 100 yards into the flag, we cannot afford to be jerky, lightning quick or painfully deliberate with the swing – we want an easy-flowing, repeatable method. This links smoothly with the world of music: classical, rock, pop and jazz.

Find that pitching rhythm

There are two main interpretations of this approach to pitching, as outlined below. The first interpretation is the exciting and emotive, operatic style, that of Seve – all to do with 'feel' and 'touch'. Alternatively, we can listen to Dave Peltz, former NASA scientist and leading golf coach.

Seve even named his golf school at San Roque in Spain 'The Natural Golf School'. This natural, almost mystical talent enables him to become 'at one' with his instrument.

Dave Peltz, on the other hand, pumps up more graphs, statistics and methodology volume in his *Short Game Bible* than there is rigging for an eardrum-busting Metallica concert at Wembley Arena.

So, where does that leave us, the audience? Only by listening to a broad band of advice, and then trying things out for ourselves, can we decide what works for us. Experiment with all pitching suggestions to discover what suits you best That said, as in the previous chapters, there is still a basic style (which has gone Platinum), and must surely be worth copying.

Right: Seve Ballesteros pitching on to the green. His unique, emotive style sets him apart from most of his fellow pros.

Playing the pitch shot

Working backwards from the putt we reach the putt-chip. With a little more wrist break and body rotation, we perform the pitch. Primed by the upper body, the arms and hands should feel all one piece with the trunk.

Basic pitch style

Nick Faldo gives a grade one simple approach to the set up and swing.

Pitch set up	Pitch swing
60% of weight on your left side	Use a three-quarter length swing – back and through
Flex your knees	Turn the upper body on a firm base – hardly any leg action
Arms feel weighted and heavy	Stay connected – arms and torso move as one

So your basic pitching style should be a three-quarters swing, gripping down the shaft a bit. Put the ball in the middle of your feet. Set the hips and feet open to the target line, but not too much, and keep the shoulders squarer the further away from the pin you are.

Above: **For your set up, position the ball in the centre of your stance with your hips and feet slightly open to the target line. Grip a little way down the shaft.**

Turn back and through

Regulating distance control

Pitching is all about distance control and it's hopeless if we boom it over the back of the green. The Scratch player hits full iron shots to pretty accurate yardage. By mathematical deduction, that 136 yards to the pin 7 iron can be struck with total confidence that it's not going to fly 156 yards by accident. On average, a Scratch woman will hit a full 7 iron 130–140 yards and a man 160–170 yards.

The rest of us look at the yardage chart telling us 'it's 154 to the pin' and do our best. The difference here is that out of every 10 balls, one will be roughly on 150 yards, the

Above: When playing a pitch shot, think 'tummy back, tits to target'. Nick Faldo, of course, says 'stomach and buttons' as he turns his stomach away from the target on the backswing and ends up with his shirt buttons facing the target – but I'm sure he could be convinced to think otherwise!

others will either be long, short, left or right of target. This leaves us with the pitch much more often than we bargain for.

Have you ever played in a pro-am and the caddie whispers, 'It's 66 yards to the front, 12 on, so you've got 78 to the pin'? Do we all know just how hard to swing to reach number 78? Of course not. The majority of us will be hard pushed to know what 100 yards feels like, and even if we do, the chance of regularly being able to drop it on target is slim. There are two ways of controlling distance:

- Length of swing (the Body and Clock).
- Force of body rotation (the Metronome).

The Body and Clock

Hacker and Club should both alter the length of their backswings and followthrough to control distance rather than trying out the Metronome (see below). Even if we only use 'two times', or two 'joints', it will give us a feeling of safety that means we know that if we swing back to '9 o'clock' and through to '9 o'clock', with the same force and rhythm, the ball will go 40 yards. This whacks up the confidence. We want that.

Altering the length of the backswing and the followthrough, and pretending that our arms are the hands on a clock, is a very useful distance control method for everyone, not just for the higher-handicap standards.

The Metronome

Match and better players might opt to vary the speed of their body rotation through impact – the further you want to hit the ball, the faster you rotate the trunk. On a metronome, the

Feel the beat

Tailor your pitch choice to the moment. Always make your mind up before you stand over the ball what type of shot you are attempting. If you are still deciding between two styles of pitch, when perched over the ball, the result will be disastrous. These all have an effect on ball position, shape of swing and choice of club.

meter taps out the following speeds for these music terms:

- Moderato: 108–120 beats per minute.
- Allegro: 120–168.
- Presto: vroooom!

Linking the speed of body rotation to the distance the ball travels comes from David Leadbetter. It is really suitable for Club and Match. David tells us to imagine you want to hit a 40-yard pitch shot with a 40 mph swing, a 60-yard pitch shot with a 60 mph swing and so on (don't hit Presto – hernia alert!).

Why does the Metronome technique suit the better standard of player? They don't have to think too much about the technicalities of their basic swing. Their golf is advanced enough to sense the difference in feel between a 40-yard pitch swing and an 80-yard pitch swing.

Opposite: **Practise swinging back and through along the hands of a clock. Thus if you swing back to 7 o'clock, your followthrough should end on 5 o'clock. The distance of the backswing should be equidistant to that of the followthrough.**

Use your eyes

Enough sight reading, take a coffee break. Free yourself from yardage charts and use your eyes. In golf's Classical period, fairways dotted with yardages written on sprinkler heads or 150-yard markers hadn't been written, and we still managed to successfully judge the length of pitches. We relied much more on our eyes.

Train yourself to instinctively know what 10 yards looks like. This comes with time and some people manage it better than others.

Once you are happy with counting in 10's for the long game, you can focus on 5-yard intervals. Every time you practise or walk to the car or pace the length of the tee is a chance to hone this skill.

Yardage charts can lie, so keep this in mind and use those bloodshot twinklers. Eye-hand coordination can be fine-tuned. If the 'middle eye', 'mind's eye' (whatever you wish to call it) can reach the point where by looking at the target the feeling of just how hard to hit the pitch becomes instinctive, then we're onto a hit.

Perfecting the pitch

By teaching the body to know what it feels like to bash 40-, 70- and 80-yard shots, we can dictate how the rest of the long game attacks the hole.

Play using known pitching distances

This is really a tip for the Match and Scratch as they are already at the level where they can control how far to hit their pitches. Imagine you are playing a par five and you could, if you really whacked it, reach the green. Play up short deliberately to 90 or so yards and then hit a full pitch with the wedge in total confidence that it flies 90 yards. Sink the putt and it's birdie time – the safe and intelligent option.

Left: Bernhard Langer measuring out the yardage at St Andrews. Distance control is vital – but train your eyes to estimate distances so that hitting the pitch becomes instinctive.

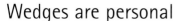

Wedges are personal

Seasoned players carry three wedges (which includes the sand iron), some having fiddled endlessly with them in the workshops, adding or removing weights, altering loft angles and generally tinkering.

Many sets of irons are fine right through to the 9 iron, then they get 'clumpy'. They are too fortissimo; too 'strong'. Too powerful, and the ball zooms off the club face before any control can be applied. Hacker and Club won't necessarily notice, but Match and Scratch will be scouring the pro shop for a Stradivarius or two. We need feel.

Each wedge is capable of achieving slightly different tones. Before allowing it to take up space in our golf bag, we must master this. The sand wedge is not just resigned to the sand. For most of us, a 60 per cent lob wedge is a waste of time – we're just not good enough to use it properly.

What you need

For most golfers, the following clubs are sufficient: a 'distance' wedge (the Utility/GAP wedge) of 52, or so, degrees (usually this is part of the main set of irons), a 'more delicate shots' wedge of 55 degrees, and a sand iron of 56 degrees.

Club selection

Use your imagination. 'There's more than one way to skin a cat'. Now, I'm sure you've heard that before. It is the golfing equivalent of 'but I always use my 60-degree lob wedge!' How many times has the anointed been brought out from the bag, waggled with a flourish, and then dumped the ball in the bunker or thinned it through the green? Gripping down on a punched 9 iron would have got you much closer – and would have been the safe option.

Ask yourself some questions:

- Do I want the ball to fly high or low?
- Do I have to clear any hazards?
- Is this uphill or downhill?
- What about the wind?
- Where do I want to end up?

Being 2 clever can catch u out

Learning from the greats: a masterclass

Annika Sorenstam

Annika plays a punch pitch much more than any other. The flight of her ball is fairly low, but holds its line right to the target. She works on the Peltz 'Golden Eight': pitching into putt lengths of 3–10 feet. These, of course, she always sinks...unlike us.

Laura Davies

Laura has superhuman strength in her forearms and wrists (for a woman). This comes in handy when blasting out of rough near the green. However, the rest of the 'fairer sex' must practise their strength exercises.

Fred Couples

Fred is so laid back, he's horizontal – look at the way he walks. He relaxes into his golf, his swing is double-cream smooth and if you watch him working on his pitches he chats to friends, looks at them, and casually glides the ball to a perfect distance without changing rhythm.

Tiger Woods

Pitching in from 70 yards out, he's like a coil wound up. This stroke marks out new territory: short, tight backswing and clean, crisp strike, then acceleration through impact so the club head points up at the sky, maintaining the loft of the club face. According to the man who coached him, Butch Harmon, Tiger spent 70 per cent of 2000, and more in 2001, working on his short game. With the amount he practises, that is more than a life's amateur hacking... makes you think, doesn't it?

Rehearsal time

Unlike bashing a full iron shot, which requires little inventive power, pitch shots identify those with a true talent for improvisation. It's time to rehearse our Full Monty pitches and Rocky punches.

Full Monty pitches

You can influence the way the ball travels through the air and how it lands on the green, i.e. the roll. These are full shots with very different landing characteristics.

Full high pitch shot landing softly

Wind spells disaster for this shot, as its penetrative powers are slight. The effect wanted is for the ball to sail up into the air, over all the 'nasties' and plop down delicately beside the pin. Knowing exactly how far you hit your full wedge is a great confidence builder as the next time 90–110 yards pops up you just reach for that wonderful wedge and give it a smooth rhythmic one-and-two (impact being on 'two').

● Set up: Open your feet (aim left – a foot) and put the ball just forward of centre. Relax the arms, making them feel close to your body. By pushing the ball forward in the stance, the hands automatically sit further back and that increases the natural loft of the club. The club face should be square to the target.

● Swing: Make a three-quarter length backswing (you will go further than that) and do the 'Tummy Back, Tits Through' swing (page 77). You should take a credit card length divot.

Full pitch with lower flight

This is useful when you have to reach the top tier of a tiered green or the green is above you on a gradual rise and you need more run on. It also keeps its line better than the high floaty shot, and is invaluable in wind. Tiger has tamed it, and Annika is its Diva.

● Set up: Slightly open your feet and put the ball back in your stance – opposite the right heel. Most of your weight should be on your left side. By putting the ball back and weight forward, you will de-loft the club face and encourage a strong forward thrust with the hands.

● Swing: Feel as though you are swinging 'around' your body. Hold the finish lower, nearer the three-quarters point. Take a credit card length divot.

Opposite: **For the Full Monty, use a wedge and take a three-quarter backswing to get the ball soaring up into the air and achieve a full, high pitch shot.**

Hannibal cut-up

'Hey, hey, I'm all cut up, uh, huh-huh, yeah, yeah...' This is a larger version of the Flip shot discussed in the Chipping chapter (see page 60).

● Set up: Open the club face and go down the grip. Open your stance.

● Swing: Unstiffen the arms and feel as though you are pushing the club away from the body on the backswing, sliding under the ball on the same line. Finish the swing with the hands up near the left shoulder. You need to follow an 'out to in' swing path.

● Lie and divot: For this shot, you need a reasonably good lie, not buried in the rough or bare. Skim the grass; there's not much of a divot taken with this.

Ball-bunker-pin syndrome ceases to cause squeaks on the score card. Having the ability to flip, flipperty, flip the ball at will, and in a controlled manner with a full swing, keeps a relaxed swing rhythm flowing and erases the chance of a nervous wristy poke into the bunker or hazard.

Rocky punches

The next three shots belong to the punch family. They all drive the ball to the target.

1 Drilled biter

2 Bash into the wind

3 Scuttle and run

With a compact three-quarters swing, we need to strike the ball on impact with *speed*. Creating speed keeps the ball on line to the target in windy conditions. The attack will be steep on the downswing.

Below: **In the punch shot, the hands and forearms pull the club across to the left. You should finish in the three-quarters position with your chest facing the target.**

Punch technique

For the set up, your hands and weight should be forward with the ball back in the stance (near the right ankle). You need a solid base, keeping your feet wide apart it it's windy.

The wrists set early in the backswing, locking the club into position, and you need to hold the wrist angle through impact. The downswing should be steep and hold through to a three-quarters finish.

This shot can be played off a bare or a

sun-baked surface. Playing out of semi-rough is fine; just be aware that you have little control over the ball's run out. The divot is ideally a credit card length.

Drilled biter: the chewy 9 iron

There is a way of convincing the ball that it will stay on direct target line without wavering; in a small breeze to medium wind the approach of the 'biter' is a winner. Also, if you are heading for a two-tiered green and the pin is up on the top level, the slightly punched 9 iron keeps the ball thrusting forwards up over that first slope and onto the target. It often works better than the floppy wedge, which relies on total judgement to reach the first bounce up on the top tier, and even the best can make a mess of that one.

Bash into the wind: half 8 or 7 iron

Links, links links – this is arguably real golf. Links make you really think. On links, more than anywhere else (and even when you hit what you reckon is the most perfect shot), some odd bounce will throw it off-line and into 'adder territory' (hisssss). A links course is alive with humour and naughtiness and can be generous at times. The 'Auld Grey Toon' plays host to golf's leader of the orchestra. St Andrews heads up a new century with the

Old Course provoking respectful 'oohs' and 'aaahs' in the Big Room. Discussions over the unlucky leap or wicked kick off one of the uncountable humps, 'buried elephants', takes place. Work on this before trying it out on course. Use the Body and Clock methods to calculate the swing length: ball flight distance relationship.

Scuttle and run: 5 or 4 iron

Golf weather can be unspeakably horrible. Skin-exfoliating rain coupled with a vertical lift off wind and the ball would be better off never leaving terra firma. Keeping the ball in play is the ultimate aim – and preferably only inches from the ground. This shot, and the one before, can obviously be applied from over 100 yards out but huge practice is required before using it.

The ability to judge a half 5 or 4 iron is useful, not just for sliding under branches. Sadly, as we like shortcuts, the only way of making sure the ball doesn't suddenly fly over the back of the flag, past the out of bounds and into the sea is to work at these shots.

Don't expect this shot to look 'pretty'. Some people may wonder if you've thinned a higher club, but then they will have chosen their 8 iron and witnessed it wafting out to sea on that light, force 9 zephyr.

Hold your finish

Practice makes perfect

As in every section of golf, intelligent practice can make the difference between someone who is talented and reaches their potential, and someone who, although equally talented, never quite makes it as they are either too busy, can't be bothered, or do not know how and what to work on effectively. Here are some pitching helpers.

There are two types of general swing drill: drills that assist the general striking of a pitch shot, any pitch shot, and drills that make specific shot practice less mind numbing.

Below: This practice drill aids the development of a positive pitching swing. You need to keep your right heel up off the ground throughout the shot.

General strike work

1 Keep your right heel off the ground as you play some full pitch shots.
2 Hit down and through the ball.
This helps to create a positive forward strike and stops us jumping up and back off the ball in anxiety just after impact.

Nick's Towel Drill

Only try this on shots under 50 yards.

1 Stick a rolled towel under each armpit and across your chest.

2 Make the normal three-quarter length swing, turning the top half of your body over a passive or quiet bottom half.

3 Try not to lose your balance.

4 Link your arms to your trunk and rotate.

Above: **With a rolled towel across your chest lodged under your armpits, make your three-quarter swing, rotating your upper body and keeping your lower body passive. Focus on keeping your balance.**

This is an excellent drill to keep the top and bottom halves of the body connected. Note that preventing unpredictable shots from zooming off the club face is what good pitching is all about.

Work on your weaknesses

Boredom busters

With all these suggestions for increasing your distance control, it is up to you to decide how many balls to hit and the yardage splits, what targets you want to hit and any implements you wish to use. Hopefully, these drills will give you some ideas.

'Chuck it in the bucket'

This drill comes from the boys on tour.

1 Put 4 empty range ball buckets in a line in front of you, spaced out at 15, 25, 35, stretched paces (an average stretched pace equals a yard).

2 Hit 5 balls to each bucket.

3 Really concentrate on how much force you need to put into the swing to change distance.

Choose your landing zone

This is two bunkers distance honing. With 10 balls, hit to land in alternate bunkers. One should be about 40–60 yards out and the other 80–100 yards. This is really for the longer shots, on the outer limits of the pitch up to the full wedge. Say, 80 and 110 yards.

Right: For the Mary Poppins drill, stick a couple of umbrellas in the ground at 20 and 40 stretched paces and open them up. These are only rough distance guides; any variables will do. Hit 5 balls to the nearest umbrella and 5 to the next and then reverse it. Hit alternate shots to them.

Amateur hiccups

Finally, there are two traits that we amateurs are prone to. Not getting the ball up to the pin happens on long putts, too; it is as if we are unsure of what lies on the far side of the pin. Daft really. The second point, I have to admit, was pointed out, rather than me thinking: 'By George! I must land the ball on a flat part of the green...'

Falling short

Falling short of the target is something the pros rarely do and when pitching in to the flag, if you run past it, quite often you will find less trouble at the back of the green than at the front. It is really a mental approach thing but varying conditions can alter this approach. For example, if playing a links in summer, with the turf hard-baked and running fast, it would be stupid to pitch the ball right at the flag as it would bounce into the next universe. Weather and course conditions play a massive role in deciding how to approach any green, as does ability. Through the green there is less trouble.

Find the flat

This is perhaps even more relevant to pitches than chipping as the chip hits the ground earlier. Hit the perfect pitch onto an uneven part of the green and you could bounce anywhere. Choose a flat landing area.

Warning!

One key note to memorize for every pitch or punch is as follows: play the pitch shot with 75 per cent swing force only. Playing any wind instrument too loud, or 'overblowing', makes the tuning go up the spout – we all probably remember that dreadful noise from school recorders! Be careful about hitting really hard wedge shots. This risks both loss of direction and of distance control – which are the whole point of the short game. Remember that this is not the power game.

Encore

In pitching and punches, keeping to a simple 'do-able' shot, is always wise. Be flexible with the mental approach to a shot. Consider a half 8 iron punch as opposed to a high-floaty wedge. Always complete the swing – even if the finish is a three-quarter punch driving the arms towards the target.

Use a 75 per cent force swing for the pitch shot

Summary

A golden rule of enjoying a rock concert is to hold on until the end for the encores, as they're often the best bit. It's exactly the same with pitches and punches – hold your finish position and count to three.

Find out what's on

It's 100 yards to the pin – what are you left with? Keep to a simple, 'do-able' shot.

Choose a gig

Visualize the shot and where you want to end up. Select the appropriate club, then use your imagination!

Collect tickets and find your seat

Set up, stand open, flex knees, even weight, soft arms, grip down the shaft.

Stand your ground

'Tummy back , tits to target' 75 per cent or less swing. Remember: this is not the power game.

Shout your head off

Hold the finish. The arms and hands should feel as one with the trunk of the body.

CHAPTER FIVE

Hazards

Hazards, such as bunkers and water, can provide endless amusement to voyeurs and pain to players. In the law of the golfing jungle, escape is paramount – preferably with as few wounds as possible. As we run through the history and topographical layout of bunkers, the main species are outlined alongside where to find them and the types of sand we have to tackle. We can then understand how to play these wild beasts.

Types of bunkers

Let's take a look at the varieties of bunker we encounter on a golf course and the different approaches they demand. Making up your mind before choosing a club and deciding what type of bunker shot is to be played, will prevent unnecessary frustration – and loss of shots.

Dangerous breeds – keep out!

Pot: Evil tight dungeon dweller. 'Bastado, Bastado, *Bastado*!'

Scrape: An excuse for a bunker, a shallow character. Do not let your guard down.

American: Friendly, often oversized – and lipless. You could be overwhelmed.

Heather-clad: Wearing a necklace of bonny heather, getting trapped in their fringes can result in strangulation.

Sod-walled ('revetted'): Often possessing a harsh regimented front; better to escape backwards than take this mean mother on, face to face. Revetting means regulated layers of horizontally packed turf strips, usually at the bunker face but sometimes around the sides, too. Turf strips stabilize an eroding links face.

Bulkhead: With railroad boards set into the ground, slightly off the vertical, you do not want to come too close to this one's front lip.

Left: Darren Clarke excels at escaping from a bunker during practice at Augusta.

Right: There's nothing more satisfying than a great escape from a bunker. Bash the sand and explode out but don't get greedy with club selection and beware the bunker's lip.

Danger zones

Bunker placement and the club you select are important considerations. We are faced with bunkers in the following locations:

Green guardians: These can be pot, American, heather-clad and revetted. A sand iron or occasionally the putter will be our weapon.

Fairway fiends: Usually placed 100–150 yards from the green, these can be lethal for the score. Landing in one often means a shot dropped. Accept that by being over-ambitious, and by not getting out, the ball may be abandoned, rotting in the bunker. Club choice is dependent on the steepness of the front, or side lip, the lie in the bunker, and how far left to go to the green (probably 9–6 irons).

Drive catchers: Perfect drive, swallowed by rabbit hole (pot bunker). Pots can be lying in wait at the corner of a dog-leg, side, or across the middle of the fairway (cross bunkers). Our greed for distance may result in permanent residence in the sand.

Sand surfaces

The sand surfaces from which we play can exhibit unique characteristics, and thus before we walk into a bunker, taking note of the type of sand and knowing how to handle it, can save one or, in some cases, many more shots.

Fluffy: Like caster sugar. It looks inviting but acts unpredictably and we must be careful not to dig in too far and leave the ball buried closer to the front lip of the bunker.

Soggy: Lifting concrete is easier. Best way with this is to nip the ball off the surface, rather than get too involved with shifting heavy clods.

Hard-baked or lacking sand: After a drought, or poor greenkeeping. It is easy to thin the ball from a lie in this stuff.

Flooded: As long as there is an inch of dry sand somewhere, you can drop the ball (somewhere else in the bunker) without a penalty and play from your Noah's Ark.

Grass: A shaggy dip. This is the bunker that was, or is yet to be. Dependent on the lie and stance, the shot will be most likely a variation of the lob (see page 53).

Aiming for bunkers

Apart from making the course visually more entertaining, bunkers can be used as targets to actually land in. This is especially useful when the options are rolling the trousers up for a dip in a mouldy pond or bribing the caddie to kick the ball out of the heather. Hopefully, the penalty is at worst one extra shot, perhaps two. Aim for a bunker as a safety net when other options are too dangerous. These include:

- Flirting with the out of bounds.
- Ponds, burns or lakes acting like ball magnets.
- Your nerves playing up.

Err on the cautious side

Right: Jose Carilles of Spain hitting out of one of St Andrews' legendary bunkers on the Old Course during the 2000 British Open.

St Andrews scaling saga

Sometimes The Greens Committee possesses such a sadistic streak that a 'players' revolt' takes place, as during the 2000 Open at St Andrews. Walking round with Tony Jacklin and Jerry Pate on the practice Tuesday, we all stood on the green-side lip of 'Hell's Bunker' and peered downwards into that merciless bottomless pit. I have never, ever seen anything remotely like it. The face was totally vertical, leading into a flat area of sand about 9 feet below. The face of it was at 90 degrees to the sand. We just stood there and laughed. If you landed within 5 feet of the face, there was about as much chance of getting out as a giraffe scaling the Eiger.

Having spent quite a bit of money, let alone man-hours on rebuilding the face of the 112 bunkers for the Open, the powers that be weren't likely to pull them down – and there was no time. They must have had a contingency plan as, after much whining from competitors, the sand was raked up towards the face of the bunker so that if you landed in it (which was highly likely, unless you answer to the name of Tiger, who in four days didn't visit one), the ball would at least roll back towards the middle.

Perfecting your swing

Knowing bunker species, sand types and where we will come across them, is all very well but will be of little use unless we work on one aspect of our sand swing: developing a controlled wrist break.

It is hard sometimes, when you want to help someone in a bunker, can see the problem and know that the solution is simple. The majority of higher handicappers would be well advised to practise some 9 pm backswing to 3 pm throughswing pitches before they go anywhere near a bunker – this exercise gets the arms used to setting the wrists at 90 degrees. It removes the elongated, body-movement dominated, floppy swing – which will rarely succeed. Here are the symptoms, diagnosis and antidote treatment for floppy swing syndrome.

Symptoms

Confusion over how the ball will react coming out of the sand is only part of the problem. What usually occurs is that Hacker and, to a lesser extent, Club possess quite willowy backswings. If this swing is taken into the bunker the likelihood of success is slim, even if the ball has a perfect lie in the middle of a gentle open trap with no lip. The resultant shot displays one of these two symptoms:
Boo! A thinned top scuttling along the base of the sand, and, as in pinball, it comes right back to you.

Below: **If you develop a crisp action over short pitches, the whole swing will become more concise and controlled, taking the terror out of sand shots.**

Hiss! A thick lump of sand, a hurting wrist and a foot forward dribble from the ball as the lax downswing thuds the face of the club towards the earth's inner core.

Diagnosis

From the take-away position to just past the horizontal, we are not *compact*. The wrists do not naturally cock and the arms sweep away in a wide ungainly arc, the swing becoming long and floppy.

Antidote

Develop a crisp action over short pitches and the whole swing naturally pieces together better. It becomes more concise. Neater. Controlled. With renewed vigour, return to tackling sand shots, and that dislike for bunker quarantine will be given a passport.

Right: **Open the club face and then grip the club without grounding it in the sand.**

Far right: **When taking a sand shot, stare at a spot a credit card's width behind the ball.**

Basic bunker brief

Follow this, and even the most terrified bunker handler will achieve success. Beyond this basic brief, particular shots require simple changes to the set up and angle of swing plane. None are impossible – even for Hacker. This is the simple bunker shot swing. If you only know how to do this one, you will get out of most bunkers. Open the club face, then grip the club. The order you do this in is very important as it ensures your club face and body are pointing in the right direction.

Set up

Open your stance, aiming your feet left of the pin. Make sure that the club face is square or slightly open to the target. Keep your weight central and your knees flexed. The ball should be opposite your left ankle. Your grip is vital. You are aiming for a shallow angle of attack from an open stance.

Swing

Stare at a spot a credit card's width behind the ball (2 inches). Relax the arms and wrists. Swing the club along your body line, back and through, focusing on turning your shoulders. Bounce the back edge of the club in the sand and don't quit on the shot. Focus on completing your followthrough... *eeeeasy.*

Alignment and ball position

On arrival in the sand, don't worry about looking silly as it is vital to construct a stable base (and emanate a confident demeanour), so wriggle your bottom as if you had an insatiable itch on the underside of your rump, and before you know it your size 10 'plates' will be sufficiently lodged to prevent wobble (this also gives us a chance to feel what type of sand we are about to play from).

As a rule of thumb, most times we play out of a bunker the stance is open. To help this, the left foot can be turned a trifle more towards the target, than the right.

Worrying about positioning the ball exactly in the correct place between the feet will not get it out of the bunker – middle will do for most shots.

Left: When hitting a basic bunker shot, be sure to bounce the back edge of the club in the sand and concentrate on completing your follow through.

Right: **Having studied the lie, figured out how to hit the shot and settled to do the deed, the most important element of the swing is to keep swinging through after you have hit the ball.**

Swing rhythm

There should be no difference between the rhythm in a normal swing and one in a bunker, so, no freaking out when approaching a sand-pit. A lightning quick jerk, slash, or, at the other end of the scale, a slow-motion playback swing is the wrong answer.

Think rhythmic: 'one a-n-d two', then 'back a-n-d through'. Do not frighten bunker occupants with any sudden jerky movements.

By working on the short pitches, the backswing and followthrough should be controlled and compact. The angle of attack (swing plane) is defined by where the ball has settled. If you end up squashed against the rear entrance, you will have to lift the club at the takeaway as if you've just touched a sleeping alligator – almost a vertical lift-off. On the other hand, if you are lying in a genteel fairway scrape, the normal swing takeaway will be fine.

Be dynamic! – always accelerate through impact

Shot zones

Now that the basic level of sand safety is explained, we can enter specific shot zones; some are more unstable than others.

With any sand shot

Let the club head do the work – the sand acts as a buffer between it and the ball. The set up dictates everything. Equipping ourselves with shot-type knowledge enables a positive decision to be made. Approaching a 'plugged' ball with the set up and swing plane for the 'splash' shot will have the same disastrous reaction as feeding a veggie burger to a carnivore (except you are less likely to be eaten).

Once the decision has been made, commit to it totally. Dithering about whether to explode the ball out of the sand or cut it up will result in neither working properly. If it's wrong, then so be it. Be comforted that, having stridently stepped into the sand, deduced that 'an explosion shot' is the one, set up accordingly and given it a good thrashing, if the ball just rolls over giggling its dimples off, two reactions are permissible:

1 Try again in a controlled, calm manner. Until it is out, don't give up. Hit the pause button after each try, then it will get out by the fifth go.

2 Quit. Retreat. Wave the white flag before attempting any shot, then either take a penalty drop further back in the bunker, or chip out sideways or backwards.

Left: **Thomas Bjorn explodes out of the sand at the US Masters. Be confident and let the club head do the work.**

Splash shots

These shots are for when the ball is lying OK in a bunker with no huge lip to clamber over. Do the waggle, settle your base with the stance slightly open and, depending on how high a face you need to clamber over, open the club face – the more open, the more 'cut up' and therefore higher the shot will fly. Bear in mind that just opening the face and not further opening the stance could cause a socket (s...hank). The two must be done in tandem.

Set up

You need a slightly open stance and club face. Pull your left foot back and turn the club face up towards the sky. Aim a thumb's length behind the ball – not too much.

Swing

Swing on the usual plane – straight back and forward look at the sand at the back of the ball. Make the followthrough as long as the backswing. Use a sand iron for maximum bounce.

Below: **For splash shots, use an 80 per cent speed swing and slide the club through the sand. Focus on your followthrough.**

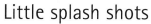

Little splash shots

A little minnow splash shot is the intimate cut-up shot. A variation of the splash, the ball sits in the bunker, right by the pin and there's not a doormat of grass to work with before the hole. The ball must fly nearly vertically, spin madly and then settle quietly.

Set up

This needs to be wide, wide open with your body set up way to the left. Open the club face as much as your dare (and more than you think). Go right down the shaft. Seve puts his right index finger onto the metal part of the shaft – don't be afraid to do this as it gives greater feel over the little shots.

Swing

Follow your body line and hold the followthrough with your hands at shoulder height. Think of swinging softly – that's what all the top pros always do.

Below: **For little splash shots, you need a really wide set up. Go right down the shaft and hold the followthrough at shoulder height.**

Glide through the sand

Explosion shots

Heading for a record-breaking handicap-reducing score and, as you approach the bunker that lung tightening sensation restricts the throat as the ball comes into view – wedged under a 30-foot high wave front lip.

If you find you are stuffed up against the front lip of a bunker and can't do the little splash shot, there is another escape route: the Explosion. Brute force will normally get you out, but there will be no control over the ball but at least it's out. This shot rids us of pent-up aggression.

Address the ball as if preparing for battle, grip the club tight and, just before you hit it, squeeze and, go on, throttle it. Keep the face of the club square, and stare transfixedly at a spot three to four inches behind the ball.

Having taken a striking position, the swing thought is to drive the club down behind the ball and forwards through the sand. The ball will rise up sitting pretty on the top of a bowl full of sand and karma will return. *Squeeze the grip* just before you hit it.

Set up

You need a solid base and a square club face (or even slightly shut). The worse the lie, use more closed club face. You need a sand iron.

Swing

Go for a steep angle of attack – a 'V' shape. Forget the follow through; use aggression. Hit down into the sand and the ball will come out running fast, so calculate for no backspin.

Above and right: **When setting up, the club face should be square and slightly shut. Adopt a steep 'V' shaped angle of attack and drive the club down behind the ball and through the sand so that the ball flies out.**

Drive the club down behind the ball

Left: Jan Stephenson hits out of a bunker on the 15th green during the second round of the 2002 ANZ Australian Ladies Masters golf tournament. The pros relish being in bunkers as they can control the ball.

Downhill stance shot

Use this shot when the ball is on a downward bunker slope, probably at the back of the bunker. This slippery customer represents the Python who assures you the bulges in his abdomen are not your brothers and sisters he swallowed during a peckish midnight feast. Failing to generate enough loft can result in the ball being swallowed by a mound of sand under the front lip. What we must do is to neutralize the downward pull of the slope by aligning our spine with the line of the slope.

Below: **By tracing the line of the slope on the downswing, the ball will come out low with no backspin and not much control. Still, it is better to get it out than stuff it under the front lip of the bunker.**

Set up

Go down the shaft and open the stance, keeping the club face square. Bend 'ze knees' more than usual and keep 90 per cent of your weight on your left side. Use a sand iron.

Swing

Setting the wrists on the backswing is very important – you'll feel a big wrist action. Clear your right hip on the way back. Follow the downslope of the bunker, releasing the right hand under and down the slope. Stay down over the ball and chase it towards the target. Let it run.

Uphill stance shot

This shot is for when the ball is on an upward slope, probably near the front of the bunker. Landing smack in the face of a bunker, where it looks like you will need five-inch spikes under your shoes just to hang on, gives you a steep upslope shot. This is the sister to the Downhiller and, in the same way, the angle of the spine sets everything up. Firm thighs are needed for this one; the right one carries the brunt of your weight. Remember that upslope adds loft to the shot.

Set up

Stand a fraction open with a square club face. Go down the grip. Use a sand iron.

Swing

Your swing should be wide and aggressive. You should hit the ball further than you judge necessary as the slope will send it up higher into the air than you expect. Keep the legs still and force the club upwards. Follow through up the slope, urging the ball up and towards the pin.

Below: **You need a slightly open stance. Go down the grip and keep the club face square. Your weight should be on the right side. Force the club upwards.**

Keep going up and through... be wide and aggressive

Plugged lies

Play this shot either when the ball has landed in soft sand, or, when it is plugged. There are two degrees of badness.

Firstly, with a poached lie, the ball is visible but surrounded by a rubber-ring of soft sand. If we can chuck the sand forward, the ball will fly out as if riding high on a pillow of angel dust. Secondly, there is the plugged lie. If you can see any part of your ball, that's a result. It is certainly not a cop-out if you dig it out with your fingers and take a penalty drop – back in the bunker where at least you can swipe normally at it.

Set up

Open the stance. Use a square club face for poached lies; hooded for plugged. Use a sand iron on soft-scoop sand; a wedge on firm sand.

Swing

A forward digging action combined with a steep 'V' shape swing and only a bit of follow through are needed here. The worse the lie, the more the ball will run (there is more sand between the club and the ball). Allow for the fact that when the ball comes out of the sand, there will be no backspin 'suck-back' and it will run and run.

Below: We all hate these awkward shots but if you follow the swing sequence shown here, you will escape. You need a steep V–shape swing with only a little followthrough.

Thump the sand with your right hand

Fairway flier

Remember that distance is your main aim, so taking the ball clean or thinning it is far preferable to a thick clotted thud just juddering over the front lip. Play this shot when the ball is lying in a fairway bunker, with a good lie and a clear (low lip) exit route. There is probably quite a distance (150+ yards) to go to reach the green.

Walk into the bunker without a club. Wiggle and sense the sand for its texture.

Take sufficient loft to clear the lip comfortably. If you reckon the green is reachable, choose one club longer than if you were hitting from the fairway. This is because gripping the club down the shaft and concentrating on an easy swing will result in the ball flying not quite as far as usual. We don't want to thrash at it and throw the balance off, as a flub could occur.

As for hitting the woods, if the ball is sitting up and there is no front lip to speak of,

Above and right: **By gripping the club down the shaft and focusing on an easy swing, the ball will fly less far than usual. Your lower body should be stable as you swing. Make sure you stay balanced.**

then a 5, 7 or 9 wood can work. Experimenting is the only way to find out if you are happy attempting this, but do so before it matters.

Set up

You need a square club face. Go down the grip. Keep the weight even and put the ball middle to forward in your stance. A sand iron down to 5 iron is safe. If using woods, the 7 and 9 are easier although better players can handle a 5 wood.

Sarah's soundbites

Stand tall over the ball. Pretending that the top of your head is attached by string to the clouds stops you ducking down during the strike and taking too much sand.

Swing

Aim for a smooth and gentle controlled swing. Keep the lower body stable and concentrate on staying balanced. Make a wide sweeping arc.

A smooth takeaway... let it fly

The in-between shots

Thirty to ninety yards from the pin are the most awkward bunker shots to judge. We have to assume that the lie in the sand is no problem and there is no hideous high lip waiting to snaffle the ball.

These shots are the most difficult to gauge and we never know exactly how this lot will react. The actual shot is not hard in itself; what is tricky is to consistently judge the distance to the pin and then translate that onto our swing. It is an ordinary pitch shot with two differences:

1 Square up the club face.
2 Put the ball back in your stance.

Set up

Keep your stance slightly open. The club face should be square. Go down the grip and keep the weight even. You need to use either a wedge or a 9 iron to help the ball run forward.

Swing

Turn back and through with a solid base. A longer and stronger swing means more distance covered.

Mid-range shots

For shots from 30–60 yards out, you can strengthen the left-hand grip. Turn the left hand a bit to the right of the normal position (assuming, as usual, a right-handed player). Doing this helps create the best angle of attack when the ball is put back in the stance. Cup the wrists = cuts the club face up = adds loft.

Below: The greater the distance to be covered, the longer and more lively the swing. Speed of swing and impetus are directly linked to how far the ball pops forward. Gradually square yourself up as you go back in distance from the pin.

Above: Turn the left hand a little to the right when you are playing mid-range shots.

Practice exercises

Just being able to handle the basic bunker shot is all very well, but if our golf is really going to go places, we should become a bunkologist, and that means following a few simple practice exercises.

Sand practice

Polishing up our knowledge of how the sand iron behaves in the sand before a score card is considered, is key. Cultivating a sense of where the club fizzes off the sand is a vital part of playing bunker shots well. Since you cannot ground the club before you hit it, you rely on good eye-arm-club-ball coordination. Judge the bottom of the swing at the wrong place and either the ball will be missed, topped or 'thud!', left deep in the manure.

Grooving the sand iron

Find a flat spot in the sand. Instead of five balls in a row in front of you to hit, put five tees perkily sitting up – a good hand stretch away from one another. Try and knock the tee out by banging a lump of sand a couple of inches behind it. Do the same with the next tee. Once you get the hang of this, try banging the tees, five in a row, without pausing the swing rhythm.

Right: A good bunker exercise is to practise hitting five tees out of the sand. Line them up in front of you and bash them out rhythmically, banging the sand behind each one.

Plugged lies

When faced with a half-buried or 'down a bit' ball, it is comforting to have an idea of how it will react when we take a thrash at it. Take four balls and line them up in the bunker with the following lies:

Ball smiling: Pleasant, sitting up.

Ball with plaster on head: Down a bit – give the ball a light tap on the head after you drop it in the sand.

Ball waving white flag: Half buried.

RIP sign over ball: Undercover.

Use the same swing for all four shots and see where they go. Do this several times.

Games to play in bunkers

1 Easy splash shot

Take 10 balls and, in the bunker, hit 'splash' shots out. All the time here you are thinking what it feels and sounds like to bash the sand, and how the sand reacts to the club. Splash is golf's most useful bunker shot.

2 Exploding out

Drop a handful of balls into a deadly place and 'explode' them out. Build up the confidence when it doesn't matter. Feel just how much force you can put behind the swing to get that forward motion and ball popping out on its cushion of sand. Hit down and try to remember how hard you hit.

3 Judging distance shots

This is one area that is rarely worked on, as most practice facilities cannot stretch their space. Find a quiet hole on the golf course and, with a handful of balls (and no-one hovering in the distance), experiment with a six iron to see how far you can hit the ball from a good lie in the bunker. Try to thin it and stay steady.

Choosing a sand iron

Every one of us has, or will, buy a vehicle. We would be mad if we just opened the wallet and paid up without investigating the engine, interior and then taking it 'for a spin' to see how it turned corners, braked and reversed. This is even more relevant to choosing a sand iron, and then entering bunkers. Using the sand iron that comes with the set is not always the best option, for you. The better standard of player will be rather particular over what size flange there is on the bottom and the overall shape of the club face. If you don't love the look of your sand iron, then get another model.

Left: Use the same length and force of swing for all four shots. Do this several times and see where they go. This exercise will help you to ingrain the relationship of force between banging the sand and ball flight on your muscle memory.

Cross-country

Just when you thought everything was going great, golf chucks your ball 'out to grass' or into the water jump. Our game's equivalent of an equine cross-country course can be negotiated with a clear round, but only if we know how to cross these obstacles. Here are some that you might encounter.

Exploding out of thick grass

If you can see the ball, that's a plus point. Thick grass wraps itself around the club head, clogging it like seaweed in an outboard motor.

Set up

Go down the grip. Put the ball forward in the stance – off your left heel. Make sure the feet are firm with a shoulder-wide stance and stare hard at the ball (or at least what you can see of it).

Swing

The angle of attack should be steep, a 'V' shape. Just before you strike, grip the club really hard and squeeze. Use your body force to push the ball forward and punch it out forward with your right side.

Right: **As the grass wraps itself around the club head it takes the loft off and tends to send the shot left. Be aggressive and prepared for this.**

Stare at the ball hard

Avoiding air shots

Sometimes your ball is balanced on a grass or pocket. It sits pretty, high up in the grass, just begging to be swiped at, and if we take an innocent thump at it, 99 per cent air will be contacted and the ball will fizz and turn and then drop even deeper onto the same spot.

When setting up, go down the grip and stare at the top of the ball – *hard*. Think: wide shallow 'U' shaped swing sweeping the ball forwards. Don't try to ground your club. This is similar in approach to a fairway bunker shot, where you are aiming for distance but can't ground the club and want a clean hit.

Perched shots

Just flown through the green and ended up in the brambles but a good foot or more off terra firma? Here, the ball may really be unplayable, and the sensible option may well be to take a penalty drop. However, if you are confident you can pull this one off, it is possible (and is extremely flash). Here's how to swipe the ball from mid-air.

Go down the grip. Use a club with little loft, such as a 7 or 6 iron. Take the club away on at the same level as the ball – a flat swing. Keep the hands and wrists firm. The ball will fly off low and shoot forwards and left.

Above: Try not to fall out of the tree; and stare really hard at the ball.

Left: If you end up stymied next to a tree root, and perhaps jammed up against the tree itself, the temptation to lash at the ball is overwhelming – and won't work. A steep swing will help the ball jump out.

Jungle

From water to jungle, 'bundi', crap, whatever it is known as, get it wrong and three or four shots can be waved goodbye to rapido.

Hitting out from a tree root

To set up, open the club face and go down the shaft to give more control. Choose a club that is not overly ambitious, probably a 9 to 7 iron. Use a steep swing to 'throw' the club face at the ball and help it jump over the roots. Do not look up early.

One-armed bandit

A right-arm only shot is pretty rare. But it only has to happen once in a major competition and you'll wish you had practised it before. The ball lands snuggled up to a tree and the only way is to hit with the right arm only.

Stand with your back facing the target. Go down the grip well and open the stance. Position the ball opposite the right toe. Use an 8 or higher club. Swing straight up and down with a pendulum motion.

Below: **John Daly plays out of the trees on the 10th hole during the first day of the Masters Tournament in Augusta, Georgia.**

Water

It is usually wise to fish the ball out of the drink, take the penalty drop and play from dry land so why do we see the pros rolling up their trousers and having a splash? With this in mind, there are two degrees of submergence: hitting from shallow water and ball buried underwater.

Hitting from shallow water

This is not an option if the ball lies more than a couple of inches under the water surface. For the set up, open the wedge towards the sky. The ball should be forward in the stance. Swing as usual and easy. The club bounces off the surface of the water, as in a bunker shot. Not much water comes out and the ball shoots forwards.

Above: **When hitting out of shallow water, open the club face skywards. Keep the ball forward in the stance.**

Right: **If the ball is totally submerged, be brave and roll up your trousers. You need a really steep backswing to generate club head speed and whack the ball out of the water.**

Buried underwater

The ball lies completely submerged. Any more than four to five inches and the score is better served by dropping out and calling it quits: water is so heavy, most of us just aren't strong enough to generate club head speed to get it out. When it does come out, be prepared for a dousing. Set up with a square club face, with the ball back in the stance. You need a steep backswing, cocking the wrists early. Swing hard down behind the ball and think 'explosion bunker shot' style.

Left: Water, water, everywhere. Shigeki Maruyama escapes the pond on the par 5 18th hole in Gotemba, Japan.

Summary

All hazards are beastly to land in; even the friendly bunker can bite us if we get too close to a front lip. Experimenting with how to escape from varieties of danger is part of the challenge of golf – and this is where confident handling with your chosen weapon is the key.

Investigate the habitat

Are you stuck in long spindly grass, wet sand or in a brook? Go for the easy escape option – make sure you get out.

Survival kit

Is it the sand iron? Will going down the grip on a 6 iron really get you out of that clump of muck? Feel confident, then strike the ball.

Preserve the environment

Post-escape, rake that bunker, put the divot back (or sand if supplied) and then the next victim who visits will not end up in your track-marks.

CHAPTER SIX

The mind game

Golf is hugely mental and what we need is 'bottle'. Refusing to give in and crumble when crunch time looms is a skill that can be learnt and developed. When a match or score starts to slip away and hole after hole is lost, we feel sick. Plugging the drain to prevent further seepage requires supreme positive mental determination – guts.

Positive thinking

Emotions and golf are glued together. Elation, depression, anxiety, anger, fear, sadness, smugness, sorrow, happiness, relief – they are all in the golf bag, but never just numbness. Half the battle is recognising the warning signs and then having a mechanism to deal with these emotions when they hinder play.

Comfort blanket

Concentration, focus, the ability to inhabit the 'Zone', blocking out distractions and staying in the here and now are all necessary to produce top golf. Today it appears it is not enough to conquer golf fears on our own. Hit any practice ground where the top pros are toiling away and amidst the coach, nutritionist, fashion designer and ball wiper is the mental stimulator. We are not all able to employ a mind guru, but by reading well-chosen material and observing what specialist brains have unearthed, we can glean enough tips to sort out the muddled amateur grey matter.

Too busy to digest any reading matter at all? Below are a couple of thoughts that will carry us through most troubles.

Action-reaction link

Golf is one of the few sports where there is a delayed physical response to a prior action. Compared with tennis, where we have to

Below: **Tiger Woods rides the rollercoaster and often gets it right. Here he shows the whole gamut of emotions from despair to elation in victory.**

return the shot over the net, or in football, where we kick to our team-mate, the golf ball just sits there and waits for us to decide when to strike it. That one factor creates potential for an attack of the collywobbles.

Spend too long over the ball once it has been addressed, and we are in danger of 'freezing'. As David Leadbetter proposes: 'Count to four'.

1 Set your wrist break on the backswing to the 90-degree position.
2 Complete the turn to the top.
3 Do the downswing and strike the ball.
4 Follow through and hold your finish.
By using this method, momentum is kept a-flowing, and that painful silence of 'Go on, get on with it and hit the thing!' will belong to someone else.

Distraction technique

Feeling nervous about that league final? Worried that tendency to top chips could blow it? This technique could help. With a little chip, think: *'Make sure I stare hard at the back of the ball and keep my hands quiet.'*

In layman's language: 'There's a butterfly resting on the green, but if I'm really quiet and calm, I can chip right over it unnoticed and it won't even move.'

By having something concrete to think about, negative thoughts are pushed away. Positive channelled focus takes the mind off making a mess of the shot.

Left: **Sergio Garcia, known for his firebrand attitude to golf, has battled with gripping and re-gripping the club at address in a merry twitch action.**

Be your own shrink

There is no doubt that psychological training can improve scoring. Whether we need to become slaves to mind games to enjoy the sport is another question, but we can all benefit from dipping into and absorbing what the champions do.

Mind prep

Preparing your mind involves zoning in. Here are the four stages you need to follow.

Stage 1: Preparing the mind

'Did I lock the back door?' 'Samantha's not done as well as we hoped in her maths exam. Perhaps it's that new boyfriend...' 'The results of that blood test come back tomorrow...' These are some of the many thoughts that may flash through our minds as we address the ball. Block them out!

One of the plus sides of playing golf for fun is that the high level of concentration required to hit the ball white-washes over our other daily worries – if we allow it to do so. Forgetting niggling anxieties in an attempt to get the ball in the hole can be a tremendous stress buster.

Stage 2: Hole leap–frog

Most of us have one hole (maybe more) on our own 'home' course of which we live in fear and regularly mess up. Say it's the par 4, water on the left, 9th hole. Our mind

automatically jumps ahead, the closer we get to it, and imagines the worst. By the time we reach the 6th, the brain is worrying about the pond on the 9th. Standing on the tee, we are mentally rolling up our trousers and splashing with the ducks. It's better to focus on the hole we're playing than to worry about the ones that are still to come.

Stage 3: Don't add up

Working out that by bogeying the last five holes we will automatically reduce our handicap heaps pressure on the final run in to the clubhouse. It is sorely tempting to peek at the card and calculate how well the round is coming along – not a wise move. Instead, break the scorecard down into sections.

Play nine holes and then nine. Treat the two halves of the course independently. Add up the score at the end of the ninth hole. Then forget it. Start again at 'the turn' and really concentrate on opening the 10th, 11th and 12th holes well. Breaking the 18 holes down into sections focuses the mind. Everyone is different and some methods work

Stay in the here and now

Right: Justin Leonard, swept away by raw emotion after holing a crucial monster putt on the 17th during his final day singles match in the Ryder Cup at the Country Club in Brookline, Boston. Leonard halved his match to secure a 14.5 to 13.5 victory over the Europeans.

better for some than others. But try this:
● Focus on holes 1 and 2 – a good start.
● Tighten the mind around the turn – fatigue causes mistakes.
● Home run – the last four holes can slip away if you're not careful. So focus on holes 1 and 2, the turn and the last four.

Stage 4: No speeches

Being in a position to bask in the glory of a triumph is a real treat. The danger is the chicken and egg syndrome. Rehearsing the speech before the deed is completed is bound to jinx the outcome. Who knows what was really going on inside Jean Van de Velde's head during his Open at Carnoustie in 1999. It was absolutely Jean's Open – until that *'dernier trou'*. Ideally, we should play the course shot by shot. Casually tapping in from 18 inches – and missing it – counts just as much on the card as escaping brilliantly out of the 'bunker from hell'.

Piggy bank the good shots

Confidence knockers

Being able to accept that we are far from perfect and not to overly chastise ourselves when a bad round crops up is vital to remaining sane. Everyone hits poor shots; it's just that the better players have fewer of them and they are less destructive. They also have the mental control to let the incident go and move on.

Toxic build up

Successively missing four footers, thinning chips or murderously shanking out of bunkers will de-stabilize our Karma. The cumulative effect of 'the nasties' can grip us to the point where we fear to step onto the first tee.

Munch and slurp

The tendency to rush onto the next shot after a disaster is strong. To break this, nibble a banana or some chocolate or have a swig of water. Really it matters not what is consumed (too much), it is the act that delays the swipe at the ball while we are still angry and upset. Those few minutes will bring the pulse rate back down and we will be able to attack the task more calmly.

Pretend it's next month

Nick Faldo advocates this. After a bad shot, fool yourself into thinking you've been away on holiday, seen 'Dr Diagnostic' and are now playing brilliantly, then hit your next shot. The difference is that he thinks in terms of a week whereas we amateurs need a little longer, as we might not play until the following week.

Making the right choice

This will have happened. Standing behind the ball, club in hand and decision made on how to approach the shot, something's not quite settled but we hit the ball anyway – with a 'wet flannel' result and a 'damn, I *knew* I shouldn't have approached it like that'.

This could be due to several things: our concentration levels have dropped and a noise or movement distracts us; the weather has altered and we didn't take notice of it; or our initial decision is worrying us. Whatever it is, do not continue to play the shot. If there is any smidgeon of doubt over the type of shot that is about to be played, direction the ball should start out on, or club selection, back off the ball.

Have a quiet ponder and 'take five'. Sniff the air. Is this really a high pitch in to the flag or a low runner? Check the line on that putt again. Go back to the PSR (Pre-Shot Routine) and run through it again.

Once committed, go for it. Mistakes are made all the time, and it will be useless if standing at address with a 70-yard pitch in front of us we are still deliberating over how to hit the shot. Decide: 'Yes, this is the right shot' and let it go.

Swing thoughts

Don't take all day trying out new swing thoughts on the golf course, especially with the group behind angrily pacing up and down. If something needs working on, do it during practice, then make a shorthand version for on-course play.

De-clutter the mind

The practice ground is our rehearsal studio. Any of us who has been in the school play knows that by the time the curtain goes up, it's too late for dummy runs. High-risk street cred is at stake, with everyone we know, admire, respect and fancy out there in the darkness. A prompter, sitting in the wings drops in the whispered words that save the mind blanking silence when dry throat, sticky lip panic sets in. Golf prompting is the concise and ordered swing thought.

Defuse yourself

Worst swing, dreadful shot, player 'nobs' it into the lake. One way to defuse all this tension is to remind what's up top that none of this really matters in the grand scheme of things and that nobody gives a damn about *your* golf except *you*. They will all natter about it in the clubhouse afterwards and then move on to either discussing their golf or whether modern windmills really do contribute economically to the National Grid output.

Right: David Duval in action during the 130th British Open at Royal Lytham and St Annes in 2001. The pros can cope under pressure in an important match with hundreds of spectators looking on as they have already worked out their pre-shot routines.

Superstitions and rituals

Only playing with balls numbered '4', white tees, a black glove, carrying the marker in the right-hand back pocket – do any of these superstitions sound familiar? Do you have your own golfing rituals?

Colin Montgomerie likes to hum the last tune played on his car stereo every morning of certain tournaments. Some players *have* to park in the same spot; others become obsessed with their order of dress or diet (Tiger's red shirt final day dress, for example). It is common sense to suggest that this is a high-risk strategy.

However, treated as fun, our quirks can add to the mystery of the sport. The downside is when we lose the favoured pen to write with or the pro shop runs out of 'our' ball number we imitate a goose with too much undercarriage attempting lift-off – and *flap*!

Nerves

An acute attack rendering the hands and arms leaden and legs jellified will descend on all of us at some time. This is one area where pros and amateurs are equal. We are all human (even if Tiger appears not to be). Being on an edge means that our adrenalin system is working and, if correctly manipulated, will produce the excitement that lifts our everyday existence – and raises our golf game.

There are always some people who can manage this more proficiently than others. Experience does not always make things easier either. A seasoned county golfer aged 40 plus might not look forward to playing an up-and-

coming 15-year-old as quite often youthful innocence is oblivious to an attack of nerves, but experience must count for something. Saying to yourself, 'I've been in this situation before and know what to do: play quietly, patiently, and it'll come out OK' really does work.

Playing in character is part of this. If, when playing in a low-pressure situation, you chat

Above: **Tiger Woods is presented with his green jacket by Hootie Johnson following his triumph in the 2002 US Masters. He always wears a lucky red shirt on the final day of a big tournament.**

Right: Even top pros can be superstitious. Colin Montgomerie always hums the last tune he hears on his car stereo on the mornings of certain tournaments.

happily away to your partner, opponent or caddie, then try and do the same when the heat is on. On the flip side, if you are the silent type, then gibbering incoherently is a give-away to any opponent that your steely outer layer is unsound and will self-combust.

Breathe easy – inhale and exhale deeply

Everyone gets nervous. We can care far too much about the outcome of the game and completely wreck any chance of playing normally by trying too hard and hack miserably.

Avoid direct eye contact

When in a focused situation and with many distractions all about, rather than make eye contact with anyone, appear to look at them but do not lock onto their gaze.

Distract yourself

There are many tricks that you can try to alleviate that edgy feeling. Tummy wobbles, hands trembling and a general unease over the ball can all be relieved if we distract our attention from the event at hand. Why not experiment with these positive measures and see which works for you?

● Count the numbers of spectators – every few holes.

● Look at the view and tell yourself you could be stuck in the office or in traffic.

● Squat down or stretch while waiting to putt.

● Smile.

● Take a deep breath as you study the shot.

● Look at your playing partner/opponent in detail – study the shape of their ears, their hands, anything!

Get a grip – golf is a game, not a ritual

Strokeplay and matchplay

There are distinct mental differences between different types of play. Whereas in strokeplay every shot counts and you can't afford to take too many risks, in matchplay you really can go for it; blow a hole and you can still win the next.

Medal (stroke) play

Every single shot counts on the card. We want to avoid a major blow up at all costs.

Be cautious

If by playing 'out of our skin', that bunker on the 7th guarding the green looks easy – don't take it on. Play to the side and take one more shot. If false confidence rears and we attempt shots that are beyond us, we will pay heavily.

Take a penalty drop

Having strayed into the meadow-thick rough, the ball is spotted and looks innocuous enough but sitting down a bit in a clump of thick stuff. Unless it can be shifted sideways or forward to safe ground, for certain, it is much better for us to take a penalty drop than to break a wrist trying to hack out and ending up further in trouble. Drop it, very carefully, for a friendly lie.

Left: **Vijay Singh (Fiji) plays safe and drops the ball after landing in the creek on the 17th fairway at the 2001 International in Colorado, USA.**

Backing out of bunkers

Come out sideways or backwards. There are times when the ball is wedged right up under a steep front lip and, however tempting to either explode it out or open the club face and cut it up may seem – the success percentages are against us. Backing out of a bunker is OK.

No heroics, please

Faced with a downhill 20-foot putt for par (or birdie if you are Match or Pro standard), it is almost rude not to have a go. But be prepared for the six-foot 'twitcher' on the way back. Better to leave heroics out in medal play.

More than one round counts

Many golfers will not have to prepare their mindset for this challenge, but for Match and definitely Scratch, a competition of two to four rounds will be in their diary, and the event will require some special preparation and stamina.

36 holes: Break every hole down to a shot by shot approach in round 1. After a steady first few holes, just remind yourself constantly that there's still another round to come. By round 2, you have either banked a good start or are in deep trouble having shot way over the handicap in the first round. If it is all under control, then just plod along quietly and when a chance appears to 'go one better', attack it. If the previous day or that morning's round was a disaster, there's nothing for it but to go all out for a real storming second score. **Note:** Quite often when the opening round is unmentionable, the second try is 10 or more shots better. Having realized you've blown it, try to relax and enjoy the golf – there's always a prize for the best individual round.

54 or, more usually, 72 holes: This is what the pros do week in and week out. The aim firstly is to make 'the cut' in order that the clubs are still swinging at the weekend – so it is important to pace yourself. There are two approaches to this:

1 If the swing is in sync and your golf feels good, all the putts are sunk easily and we can do no wrong, then it will be a joy to play for four rounds and it's then a question of loving every moment.

2 If, however, it is just an average round on day 1, then the graft truly begins early on day 2. Clambering up the leaderboard is the aim to be in a reasonable position for the weekend 36 holes. Round 3 chugs along, with the focus on not making any real bloomers and to pick up shots when opportunities arise. Although not in the top tranche for the final round, by reminding yourself that the majority of competitors will be having their 'ups and downs' too, the pressure is taken off and you'll probably do better than you think.

Lighten up – it will reflect on your game

Matchplay

Some people hate matchplay. For others, it is the medal format they can't cope with. We can champion both, but they are very different beasts.

Go for it

Risk taking is at the core of good matchplay. Judging when to gamble with that slightly bare lie is like overtaking in the fast lane when you can spot a tractor bumbling towards you – get it wrong and the bonnet will be covered in silage. There is a danger of becoming wrapped up in what our opponent is doing and, in the process, forgetting our own game. When they suddenly start sinking everything from off the green, chipping in and changing their name to Seve, a fog descends upon us and we rush our routine.

Play the course, not the opponent

This time-honoured piece of wisdom is so often forgotten. When faced with Houdini, if we pretend they're not with us and work on playing each shot and each hole to our satisfaction, the onus will be on them to outwit both the course and us. Make them win holes.

Don't try to match them shot for shot

By playing the course and not attempting to match the player shot for shot, we should put ourselves in a situation where holes have to be won. It's easy to lose the plot and waste shots. By loose play and silly mistakes, we offer up holes that our opponents should not win.

Right: **Paul McGinley hopes his Irish luck sticks with him as he attempts a miracle shot during the Qatar Masters.**

Right: Even when your opponent is breathing down your neck, concentrate on your own game. Here Colin Montgomerie tries to put me off but I dig my heels in and stare straight ahead.

Handicap matches

Better players should win. However, giving away a large number of shots to the opposition heaps on pressure to play well, and a few minor glitches can transform a sure bet win to one of total incredulity as the favourite is crushed.

Team play

Some of us are better team players than individual gladiators. Putting aside our personal aims and focusing on the team can free up our natural competitiveness. We can transfer this mentally during a tight individual 'head to head' match by reminding ourselves that this triumph is not for ourselves but for the club, county or country.

Some golfers, who are often difficult characters, can contribute better in a team environment. Most matches have a singles format and a player with an unusual habit, such as slow play, can be the hidden weapon in your team's armoury. The best contribution that they can make is to focus on winning their own match, thereby bringing home the bacon for you all.

There is room within team golf for naturally bonding players and loners. The outcast may turn out to be one of the staunchest team supporters and winners when given the chance to prove themselves.

Fretting about letting the side down will do nothing for the overall result. Trying your utmost to win your own match is the best thing that you can do for the team.

Risk taking is the core of good matchplay

Generosity

This is almost a game within the game. The fastest way to create enemies is to begrudge an obvious 'gimme'. Anything inside the length of the putter up to the grip (the metal bit, unless it's hickory shafted), should be picked up and given.

Giving putts

Gamesmanship enters when you leave the putt a foot from the hole and are asked to mark it, rather than 'pick it up for one more' or 'you can have that' or 'that's OK'. Having left a ten-foot putt 'dead', it is niggling to be expected to hole out. Suddenly, one foot becomes four and the creeping doubt of a possible miss whispers up from the hole.

Sometimes there are exceedingly short putts that merit holing out. One of the nastiest is the downhill, left to right, snaky two footer. Expect to be given nothing.

Rather than the casual tap in, in the long run it will pay off to settle the stance over the putt, have a good look at the hole, draw the imaginary line to the hole from the ball, and then smoothly perform a putting stroke.

Flag holding

It's always worth checking before the ball is dangerously close to dropping in that the flag will come out – it can get stuck. (If the ball goes in from on the green, with the flag in the hole, you incur a penalty shot.) There should be no flag flapping. Unless we are vertically challenged, most flag tops are reachable and there's no excuse for not furling it in our palm.

Pin out or in?

Many seasoned golfers don't realize that even if they are off the green they can have the pin held – or even taken out. The pin can stop an overpowered ball scuttling into the bunker on the far side of the green. However, it can also deflect a chip or a putt that might have otherwise dropped into the hole.

A positive attitude is emitted when you remove the flag yourself or ask for it to be taken out. Just don't bluff. If there's a real chance of 'lipping out', then do it – but if the ball is more likely to scamper into the bunker on the far side of the green, then the pin should remain stuck in the hole.

Confidently striding up to a putt that lies off the green and then pulling the flagstick out sends the message to the opponent that 'this one is going into the hole'.

Rebounds

Balls possess homing instincts and bashing another ball already on the green, when chipping or putting from off the green, results in the stationary ball being pushed closer to, or further away from, the hole. Having agreed where to replace the dislodged ball, back it goes to its original position, for free.

The game plan

Deciding on a course of action for 18 holes affects the long game in a big way and the ripple effect can be felt closer in to the flag.

Thought training

Before venturing out onto the golf course, we should train our thoughts and then stick to them. For instance, if we wake up in the morning feeling edgy about bunker shots, one solution is to promise ourselves that if we are unsure of getting out of a bunker we will hit out backwards or sideways and stick to that decision on the course. By controlling at least one type of shot in our game, we can grip the reins and the ball knows who is the master.

Since the short game is largely one of confidence (once we have learnt how to manufacture the shots), cultivating the ability to dictate different situations is vital.

Think before driving

Before driving that first ball, always stop and think. It takes only a few minutes, and thinking the game through will put us in the right frame of mind for golf – even if the results speak otherwise.

Right: Decide on your game plan and stick to it. Miguel Angel Jimenez in full control at the Ta Shee Golf and Country Club in Taiwan.

Left: Nick Faldo designed this amazing course layout at Chart Hills Golf Club in Kent. Before you play a round, let alone a shot, stop and think about the course construction and how it will affect your game.

Course construction

This can be brought into action on our home course or on a competition course where we have had a practice round (or two) and have worked out how the course is set up, i.e. the pin placings, speed of the greens, depth of rough, hidden hazards, dog-legs and blind shots.

The better the standard you are, the more risks you can take. If you are in love with your new driver and it seems to be the perfect club in the bag, then hit that. Just bear in mind that the driver is statistically harder to control than some of the less 'flash' clubs. Depending on your standard of play, there are different ways of treating the mental approach and you need to adapt your play accordingly. Better players possess better course management.

Tee shot decisions

Having studied the course, there will be some par fours that are better served by teeing up with something other than the driver to hit the right shot for the hole. This may mean a 5 iron off the tee to find the 'wide' part of the fairway or a 5 wood to avoid a bunker – match the percentage shot to the lay of the land.

Tee up to suit the hole

Lashing with a wedge on the tee would be silly, but if the driver is off the boil and a 3 iron is hazardous to your playing partner's health, why not take a higher numbered wood, or a 4 or 5 iron and relax into your shot? The amount of distance lost will mean little when the ball remains in play.

Always stay in control

Emotions

Even if you're seething underneath, retaining your serene outer shell fools the rest of the world into believing that these disasters don't matter to you, as your next shot will be one from the Ballesteros miracle bag.

Avoid physical outbursts

Wrapping the putter around a playing partner's neck or slinging it into the branches of a tree will only result in looking immature.

Try smiling and take your time

This is not as hard as it sounds. When a horror shot tests even the most phlegmatic of characters, force a smile. Likewise, refuse to be thrown into desperation in a bunker. The temptation to hack into the sand manically is hard to resist, but by pausing for a minute and stepping out of the hazard to swish the club a few times, the build up of pressure is released before something ugly happens.

Ignore blow-ups

There is a knack to avoiding the ripple effect of a playing partner's volatile temperament. When they four putt for the 'nth' time, our concentration will be affected because their golf will go into lift-off. Meanwhile, we have to hold a score together. It's very frustrating when the person you're playing with suddenly transforms into the epitome of geniality – and all because the pressure is off them.

In a matchplay situation, there is always a tendency to copy what an opponent is doing, but this risks not only imitating the good but also following them into the woods, when really we should grind away at our own game. If they are making a real hash of it, sympathy can be left at the 19th hole. Never, ever relax and coast. Three holes up with six left to play is still not safe.

Deal with disappointment

There is nothing worse than letting slip a match we know we should have won. The last thing we want to hear from anyone, even if it is well meant, is: 'Never mind, you did your best'. The worst faux-pas is usually uttered by somebody who has never experienced the desolation of wanting something badly, almost getting it and then blowing it: 'It's only a game'. Learn to deal with disappointment.

The win

This is where we are all equals, no matter what standard we are. Winning feels the same to everyone. That light-headed sensation produced by the body's output of endorphins is also

Retain your cool, no matter what

extremely tiring and you can expect to feel flat. This applies just as much to a business deal, a performance on stage or any 'high' out of the ordinary in daily life. Having won the cup, made the speech and probably had one too many celebrating, the morning after – or, more likely, days two and three after – will feel bland and dull. We all know what it's like to come back off holiday and return to work. Winning is similar and more exhausting.

Do anything but don't play golf

The most dangerous thing to do, having won and played above our usual standard, is to go out for a few holes with a friend. The levels of concentration heightened by competition will have vanished. Unless we can accept that the golf will be loose and floppy, it is usually better to wait for a few days and, instead, accept the accolades, write the thank you letters and give yourself a break.

Left: Sergio Garcia of Spain is jubilant as he birdies the 18th hole to send the championship to a playoff in the final round of the Mercedes Championships at the Plantation Course in Kapalua, Maui, Hawaii.

CHAPTER SEVEN

Teaching us

Why do we all need lessons? A good technique is fundamental to successful golf. There are many ways in which we can learn to improve our golf. The teaching world now has technology to help us amateurs enjoy a deeper understanding of the game. Let's have a look at the how's, why's and wherefores of golf teaching.

Lessons are good for me

It is a sobering experience to witness the world's top players grafting away 'at school'. Their diligence in the presence of their coach is humbling. They are there to learn and work things out. We could all do well to soak up this behaviour.

Have regular lessons

Many friends, some not so proficient players, think they know it all. Suggesting they book a lesson receives a derisory snort – just as their driver plunges another ball into the deep 'bundi'. Taking lessons and practising regularly should be considered normal, sensible and crafty. If a league table of nationalities of golfers who take note of this existed, the UK would be skulking at the bottom. Top are the Americans, Asia is next, and Europe after that. Brits have always prided themselves on being 'amateur' at sport (even if this attitude is passé); it's that old underdog scenario. Quiz any Pro who has taught abroad and they will openly admit that Brits are the least likely to work on their golf in a professional manner. We are improving though.

This observation applies less to those of us who have the modern approach, and also those who decided early on that 'we might be quite good at this', some of whom will end up in the Match, Scratch, or even Pro categories.

A logical progression would suggest that if we take regular lessons and work on the game frequently, we should get good at it. Sadly, that 'ain't necessarily so'. We will, however, optimize any talent we may have. Correct maintenance will improve our golf.

Types of lesson

There are two types of golf lesson:
1 The swing check – the golfing version of a dentist looking for cavities.
2 Specific shot learning – this is chemistry lab experimentation. It's so much easier to grasp a technique when it's actually you that 'grows the blue sodium chloride crystal'.
Privacy and peace are wonderful luxuries, which enable those few snatched minutes of true focus to make permanent ink prints on the golfing brain. Unless we allocate regular sessions in our diaries, any potential lurking in us will be banished to the bottom of the pile of dirty laundry. Lessons are worth it – with time to practise what's been learnt.

Don't let your talent fester

Pros are the best teachers

Part-time golfers are guilty of not listening but over-analysing and then giving their 'two pennies worth' to their peers. We all meddle with each other's technique. Even the top pros bunch up and swap ideas, look at each other's swings and try out new twists. They can do this – they know what they're doing.

Beware of cribbing from high handicappers. The more we play, the lower our handicap should drop, and the better equipped we are to help a friend. It's best to leave the basic swing mechanics to the pro but even a low-handicap amateur can spot problems, such as a change in rhythm or set-up. Identify the problem, but take care as to exactly what is recommended as a solution. Wrong or woolly advice can be confusing and destructive.

Pros have been trained to teach; most amateurs haven't. Lessons should be a combination of learning new elements and revision seminars. What you do find is that the longer you play the game, certain repeatable swing faults creep in. If a playing partner points out 'you are a bit quick from the top', you will probably recognise your symptoms and, hopefully, having been taught well, be able to fix the problem. A good tutor is one who explains how and why things work. This can take several attempts for the brain cells to soak up; if one approach doesn't turn on our lightbulb, then 'teach' has to keep trying until the 'Oh, I get it now' cognition smile spreads across their student's face.

Right: Nick Price, Jim Furyk and Greg Norman are agreeing with the legendary coach Butch Harmon. Even the top pros are willing to learn and will listen to their coach's advice.

Find the right teacher

All teachers have quirks in their instruction methods, even if they come from a 'teaching factory' (PGA, US PGA, etc.). The fundamentals of the golf swing may be engrained in them to be the same, but their own character, their beliefs and which part of the game they're really into, will personalize that interpretation.

In varying degrees, some tutors will be better at long game honing and would rather leave the short shots, or putting, to someone else. This shouldn't really be the case, but it does happen. If, for example, bunkers are proving a real headache for you, and your usual tutor doesn't seem overjoyed to help (or you don't understand their explanations), then there are three options that you should consider:

1 Go to someone else.

2 Read a manual or magazine.

3 Watch a video.

Telepathy

Chemistry between the coach and player is vital. You need a good rapport with your local guy so save up for masterclasses with Dr Golf, video them and then, back in the comfort of the home driving range with a friendly face to discuss it and build on, your season's strategy will flourish.

The better the standard of golfer, the more able they are to judge whether the 'training session' with a new coach worked for them or not. If someone tries to pull apart your swing, incurring years of extra study, before you enrol in their programme, think very hard whether you are willing to put the time in – or whether you are happy with what you've got. It is so easy to be sucked into technical wizardry.

There is also the case of the good teacher but a character clash with their pupil. As in form teacher and 'black sheep' of the class, get out of there fast. You are paying them!

Golf is a physical game, but one where

Above: 'OK, Colin, if you promise to behave, then I'll have a look at that loop on your backswing.' 'Thanks, Lead, I'll be good, honest.'

Build a rapport with your coach

Above: **Where would Tiger Woods be without Butch Harmon? He has helped him to nurture his golfing career and has always been there for him with constructive advice and reassurance when things don't go as well as they should, even for the Tiger.**

small adjustments make huge differences. The teaching of it should be physical, too. Living with a 'nanny state' paranoia over physical contact between the tutor and their pupil (whatever sex or age) can hinder the golf swing's development. Sometimes the only way to really 'get it' is when the teacher literally places your arms and body in the correct positions. Fortunately, video analysis has really helped with this, and it should be a regular check habit to have the swing filmed and then explained to you.

Combating coach–player distance

An incredible example of chemical bonding is the relationship between Karrie Webb and her coach Kelvin Haller. Karrie utilizes phone, videos and the internet to discuss her swing regularly with 'Hal' in Ayr. He ponders over minor alterations and then emails or phones with the fix. Ayr is beyond the map; try Queensland and then 25 hours of driving through wallaby country to Crocodile Dundee territory. Haller only makes visual contact with his star pupil perhaps twice a year but questioning Karrie about why she goes back to Kelvin risks the steel jaw look that pushed her to the No. 1 slot.

Learn in the 21st century

Today, technology enables us to analyse clinically. Where there is a weakness, whether it's in the swing or the short game, we can turn it into a strength.

Golf has irreversibly changed. You can email your coach with a problem and get the solution back through the 'ether' in minutes. Getting a swing video analysed or trying out a new driver with a laser averaging out exactly how we hit it, can save considerable time and money trying out an unsuitable club or shaft.

We can all take advantage of this. No longer is space technology assistance only in the domain of those who can afford it. Taking home a swing CD or a basic version of a golf swing software package is now quite cheap. A variety of software programmes exists and you should research the available products.

Enigma 4 amateurs

Code breaking into palatable language is a job for the pro. For instance, ball speed should be about double that of the club head speed to maximize distance. The perfect launch angle does exist. It is possible that that fancied new driver actually sends the ball a shorter distance (distance measured being the length carried in the air only) than our original club.

Having interpreted all this data, the pro can suggest the best club for us. Taped-up, it can be taken out on the course for a test drive in the knowledge that we've been given a better chance of improvement than if we had opted for the one that felt good in the shop.

What does technology mean?

It might just mean that in a few years' time the average Club standard golfer will be a better standard and will, without doubt, have more understanding of the golf swing. There is probably a limit to many further advances in computerized teaching aids. For all this computer help, there's still one human element that makes all the difference: the teacher. Robots, lasers and CD Roms will never totally replace ape conversing with ape.

What about the Kidz?

Speeding up the learning process by immediate video analysis of the next 'wonder kid' heaps pressure on to be the best – fastest. To keep up (if the aim is to reach the top), our youngster has to begin with a professional attitude when just out of kindergarten.

The days when an eight-year-old was handed a club, shown the basic grip and left to their own devices to find a natural swing, are dodo dead. The truly rhythmic player with a quirky swing, Ballesteros 'get-out-of-the-jungle' imagination and greenside magic is in danger of being replaced by the Tiger clone.

Late teens and 20s are already up in pro lights – Ty Tryon, Luke Donald, Paul Casey, Adam Scott, Paula Marti, Grace Park, Si Ri Pak. Behind them are thousands of young hopefuls.

Right: Here's the great David Leadbetter helping me to improve my golf swing at his stunning golfing academy in Florida. Some of the most famous names in the game seek out David's advice and coaching expertise.

Do I need masterclasses?

The one thing the next generation of potential superstars have in common with the rest of us is that at some point in their careers they will seek out a coach who can get them to the next grade. Golfing gurus are in great demand right now and some nestle in exotic locations.

Keep faith in yourself!

Leave London, and just eight hours later you can be on Grand Bahama with the man instrumental in Tiger's ascension into golfing heaven, Mr Harmon. Butch, the man who re-built 'that' swing in 1997, launched his second golf school in 2001, his first being in Las Vegas.

Having glared at the split screen computer image with your swing on one side and Tiger (oh, Mr Perfect) on the other, the marked differences will, of course, be blinding, but the overall effect is like an insulin boost to the golfing system. Of course, we don't need to travel the Atlantic to see our swing on a computer. Back at home, when a friend asks, 'So, what was it like, what's he like, what did he have to say?' think two words: short game.

Work on the short game, perfect the short game, become fascinated and addicted to the short game, fall in love with the short game, and play short game games with your friends.

Why? Because if we can't get the ball up to the hole and into it regularly and reliably, then we'd better take up another sport.

Superstar player academies

There are quite a few of these. Nicklaus has his, Player has his, and look in the back of most golf magazines and there will be lists of 'golf schools'. Some players appear to lend their names to these establishments and then have little to do with them after the opening ceremony and occasional PR stunt; others really do preach how their superstar deals with golf and try to pass on that extra special tit-bit from their master.

Camp David

David Leadbetter is golf surgeon to so many stars – with Nick Faldo being the most famous Old Boy. 'Lead' hangs out at his spanking new Academy at Champions Gate in Orlando. Ernie Els, Michael Campbell, Mark McNulty, Nick Price, et al. – they all come for a check up. New blood is healthy, too. Ty Tryon, the twin Wongluekiet sisters, Justin Rose and what seems like half of collegiate America works on their game there.

'Laid back Lead' makes learning and swing perfecting enlightening and fun. Being keen

Eat, sleep, dream the short game

to go to school is not just for swots – and a golf academy set in 'tan-tastic' weather is no longer pure indulgence but an affordable priority. Teaching aids and hi-tech wizardry in an immaculate Florida environment inject neat 'I must work at this game' hormone into any of us who may possess the golf practice equivalent of an underactive thyroid gland.

Co-education

Certainly a female pro will understand the physical differences between a masculine and feminine swing, but a male pro can study that, too. What can be learnt from the girls on tour is that they rely less on brute force, due to lack of upper body strength, and more on rhythm. We can all do with more rhythm. What is unexpected, however, is that the short games of women tour pros

Space age specialist

Golf can be as scientific as you want it to be and Dave Peltz, who was a NASA scientist for 15 years before he concentrated his efforts on analysing the short game is arguably the top gun. Dave holds the golfing equivalent of all the car engine manuals ever printed and can draw a perfect graph of gasket performance versus engine age. Dave's golf schools and books, entitled 'Bibles', enlighten the masses in the hidden art of the short game and putting.

are not as good as their male counterparts. Men have better spatial awareness than women and are more able to focus on working on a particular shot – they are more single-minded (no map reading jokes allowed!). What matters is compatibility, not our sex.

Right: **This is golf coaching at its most enjoyable – on the beach with the amazing Butch Harmon, learning how to do it like Tiger.**

Left: Learn from the greats, as I am here with the legendary Nick Faldo. After our session, Nick practised for two hours... in the rain. Now, that's dedication for you.

Should we pay school fees?

Not everyone can afford to be taught by the best coaches. Matching up tutor and pupil successfully is more important than seeing 'that special person' several times a year. Fortunately, systems are in place to spot and develop young talent.

If your offspring shows promise aged five, there will be Saturday morning sessions at a driving range, golf club or school. After that,

there's a competent network of administrators from County to National level. Contact the County Junior Organiser (CJO) for guidance.

There is usually some figure in our lives who has made a positive impact early on. In golf, this senior–junior relationship is very relevant. Golf clubs can be daunting places, full of rules, dress codes and older people and it's easy to make a complete hash of one's debut on a golf course. Without a friendly mentor to take us under their wing, our experience of golf clubs can backfire.

Novice 9 holes

Clutching the cup, aged 10 – having just sped round our first 9-hole competition, carding a 63 – feels like winning the Masters. Feeling special is what it's all about, especially in golf where there are so many elements involved in completing the task.

Getting off the blocks

If there are no parents, elder brothers and sisters or kindly interested souls to help, it is unlikely your junior will get off the starting

Left: Everyone has to start somewhere and the Great White Shark Greg Norman enjoys a round of golf with his son. Although most kids don't have a famous pro for a father, they can find friendly mentors.

blocks and keeping 'it' going, year after year, is just as demanding, not only on their time but also on anyone who takes an interest in them. Golf is not a mainstream team-involving sport; it can be quite isolating and practice can be lonely – especially when everyone else at school is off playing team games and you are wielding the wedge and a bucket of balls on a golf range somewhere else.

Within a golf club, there is usually a character who puts in unpaid hours and hours of telephoning, prize buying and car ferrying – and all because they believe in junior golf. It is only a couple of decades later, when the junior has grown up, and if they are not just playing but somehow involved in promoting the game, that they realise the importance of such a person. How on earth does one repay that? By trying to keep the complexion of junior golf free of acne. By combining traditions, rules and etiquette, modern technology, updated fashions and borrowed fun attitudes from other sports, we form a mix that gives us 21st century golf – golf we are proud to wave the flag for.

To join a golf club (unless we join as a junior member) we must have a handicap, and to get a handicap we need to put a certain number of cards in, and it is easier to put cards in if we play regularly on a golf course we are familiar with.

There are quite a number of 'pay and plays' where we can pay the green fee and 'suck it and see' without much financial damage. The hitch comes when we are hooked and want to progress. Practising at a driving range is good, but rarely are there short game facilities of note. They also fail to teach us about getting the ball in the hole, how to read a golf course or course etiquette.

The poor student

Joining a golf club can be ridiculously hard at any age. In some clubs, the older and poorer standard we are, the less interested the committee is. Some have realized that impoverished students over 18 can retain threadbare bank accounts way longer than expected. Many amateur golfers are still on the bottom rungs of the income ladder when they knock on 30. Having spent all that time and energy on encouraging juniors, what's the point of losing them because the annual subscription is too high and it is not financially viable for them to play regularly? Playing half a dozen times a year by green fee won't provide golf with a backbone of youthful amateur club support.

What about the over 21s?

The rest of us have a choice. We can jet off to work on our short game. Wherever there is a worthwhile golf resort, there should be a spa, tennis, shopping, crèche facilities and possibly beach to keep the family amused. Amateur golf is meant to be fun, and fun is meant to be for all the family. Back at home, golf clubs are slowly becoming more family friendly, too.

Let's nurture young talent

Keep the amateur flame burning brightly

The governing bodies of amateur golf have acknowledged there is a problem with fostering top-flight golfers in the 20–40 age bracket – people in the Scratch plus (0–3 over par) range who have had county and country competitive experience. Does this matter to amateur golf? Absolutely, it does.

Without people who have had experience in battle at the top of the amateur scene, there will be no team captains who can relate to what their gladiators are going through, and there will be fewer people to serve the amateur game on governing committees, who have a working grasp of what they're talking about. This filters all the way down to the high handicappers and no handicappers.

This draining of talent has occurred as the pro ranks have swelled. The majority of players who have represented their country will either have turned pro, or be thinking of it. Every amateur sport has become more professional in manner, and golf is no exception. This suggests that all available funds are allocated towards those people who show promise and dedication to their golf.

These recipients are the talent whom the selectors agree will be the best players for the national and international teams. The only hitch is that they will nearly all turn pro. There is nothing wrong with that but there is a dire need to hold onto and encourage those players who decide to remain amateur for life.

Addressing this situation, the women's game is following the men's example with the inaugural British Women's Mid-Amateur Championship for the over 25s in 2002. There is also increased interest with higher entry figures for Seniors amateur championships (over 50). Golf is one of the few sports where we have the opportunity to achieve county and country honours later in life.

Work hard... play harder

Left: Justin Rose moved swiftly through the amateur ranks to make a successful career for himself on the professional tour.

The 19th hole

Why on earth do we play golf? For some of us, it's just a form of stretching the legs at the weekend, to others a vital social club. Venturing onto the fairways can enrich our lives and, in some cases, literally keep the heart and soul ticking.

Can you think of any other sport where professional athletes at the peak of their physical and mental prowess can share the same pain and pleasure as the ordinary swinger? We can all miss putts. Shanks happen to everyone (Constantino Rocca), chips are flubbed (Sandy Lyle) and there's even a splashdown (Jean Van de Velde).

Who says that Tiger feels more tingling down his spine when he drills a 3 wood to 2 inches than I do when I catch one just right? Clobbering the ball perfectly 100 yards means just as much to a beaming eight-year-old as banking a cheque does to the Tour pro.

Oscar Wilde famously said that golf was 'a good walk spoiled'. For some, probably it is, especially when a case of violent snap hooks take over. Golf can torment. However, there is no other sport where a gentle wander over assorted countryside soaking in extraordinary views is on offer – and possible for all ages.

Perceived by many as a middle-aged pastime, golf is much maligned. Not high impact, not fast aggression nor a contact sport, it provides complete competitive satisfaction. Nerves are jangled and surges of adrenalin are all in there. I've felt them.

Golf is a mostly self-governing game.

There is little point in pretending to be better than we are, or guarding the handicap – we will be found out. We must aim to become as good as we can. It matters not a jot if that means playing to 42, 28, 7 or plus 3.

If we play golf in the manner it was intended, we experience graciousness in triumph and defeat. Being magnanimous in giving your opponent that three-foot putt that clinches the match when they had 'two for it' anyway is an elegant way to bow out.

Golf can be a game that other people play. We could stay in the office or scrub the kitchen floor and...

We will never strike the ball like the pros do,
We will three putt,
Four footers will cause heart murmurs,
Airshots, shanks, tops and duffs will be in
   our repertoire.
Greed will cost us shots,
Frustration, disappointment and
   embarrassment are ours.
We will fear bunkers,
Rules will confuse us,
Etiquette faux-pas will trip us up,
We will give up golf.
We will take golf up again and love it –
   and hate it – and love it.

Index

Dedication

To Angela Uzielli – an amateur's amateur

Sometimes in life an extraordinary human being leaves an indelible mark upon you. Angela Uzielli was such a person. She achieved much in her long golfing career, winning the British Championship in 1977 and playing in the 1978 Curtis Cup. She won the English Amateur Championship and the British Seniors Championship at the age of 50 – all without losing her sense of fun. Angela died very suddenly in 1999. After three tributes in the British broadsheets and a memorial service, overflowing with friends, we bid her farewell. Golf will never see the likes of her again.

As her legacy, there is now a fund for 'bursaries for young English girl Amateur golfers who want to develop their game while studying at university or college'. On-going support is raised by 'Angela golf days'. So far, six girls are benefiting.

Angela championed people and everyone became her friend. We all know someone like Angela, whatever area they decide to pop up in – it's lucky for golf that she chose to waggle a driver. When we first met she made me laugh. My friend and mentor on and off the golf course, she was my county foursomes partner for several years and my competitive nature was honed from endless battles with her at the helm. Her impish humour and love of a good gossip while never being unkind and always thinking of others is ingrained in my own life ethic. There will never be another Angela in my life.

Author's acknowledgments

My thanks to everyone in the amateur and professional golfing world who has had the patience and sense of humour to put up with a 'mad redhead' pestering them for advice, information and photos. To Bally, Oakley, Adidas, Salomon, Taylor-Made and Nike for cool kit. To team Harper Collins for hanging in there. To Heather and Rolando at SP Creative Design for their ability to break the mould. To Ed Victor for taking me on: 'Try and behave, Sarah!' And Ann of Ann Scott Associates PR without whom this project would never have happened. To my mates: Rich ('greeeen, Percy'), Fon, Talbs & Emma, Suds, Tim, Grahame, Bill, Pete, Ed, Kelt, Woo, A and especially Wff – for propping me up. To TomTom, Molly and Noah for 'hitting the spot!' To Giles, my ex-husband, for being a rock. Most of all, to Mummy, Daddy and TJ for always being there whatever heinous crimes have been committed. To Dave 'DC' Cannon for his award-winning photography and laughs. Lastly, to Cornwall for giving me strength.